Happy + Enlighten!... reading!

love Always,

5/2018

Paramitas, the Gathering of Many Rivers

Paramitas, the Gathering of Many Rivers

Michael Edward Owens

OPEN HEART BOOKS

For more information, visit www.thewayoftruth.org.

ISBN: 1-4392-1137-X

Library of Congress Control Number: 2008908614

To order additional copies, please contact: BookSurge Publishing www.booksurge.com 1-866-308-6235 orders@booksurge.com or Amazon.com

~ Acknowledgments ~

My special thanks to Carrot, for her assistance and collaboration in the gathering of these words.

And for the others, who know who they are, my deepest gratitude and blessings, always.

~ Sri Michael Owens

~ *Table of Contents* ~

~ ♥ ~

~ Introduction ~

Greetings to all sincere seekers of the knowledge and wisdom of God! This book explores virgin territory of spiritual subjects never before given written form; it offers a glimpse into universal secrets and truths that have rarely been revealed in the physical world of humans. I wanted to create a handbook for the God seeker who is ready to take the next spiritual leap forward into the unknown realms of universal wisdom. There are many "keys" hidden within the words of this book that will unlock places in the human consciousness that will stimulate further understanding and interesting Universal Soul Movements via contemplation.

Paramitas is the gathering of many rivers that come from the farthest reaches of the God Worlds to unite into an ocean of prolific spiritual knowledge and understanding that can be accessed by the sincere seeker of truth. It embraces One Universal Heart and the Oneness of our Creator. May you find your key to greater spiritual awakening and bold adventures in the pages of this book.

Blessed be.

~ *Sri Michael Owens*

~ Chapter One ~

The Sound of a Different Drummer

~ ❤ ~

When soul listens to the subtle messages of its own heart, it is hearing the Voice of God, because this center of its being is designed to be the receptacle of Divine Love. The participants of the Light and Sound of God are taught to develop the qualities of the selfless heart — and this is the "true heart" that beats within the human body.

~ ❤ ~

The purpose and effects of initiations in The Way of Truth

Initiations are given as a rite of passage to each soul who is ready to take the next step forward in his or her spiritual unfoldment. Each initiation represents a milestone in the soul's life and indicates how far he or she has come and how far he or she has yet to go to reach the shores of the Sea of Love and Mercy. An initiation is a spiritual diagram that can be read by the Masters to see where souls are in their development and how they can best serve in the forward movement of the Best-Laid Plans of this Sugmad (also known as God; *see* Glossary.)

The purpose of the initiations in The Way of Truth is to give each participant the greatest opportunity for spiritual growth that is available at this time in the history of mankind. The effects of initiations are to forever cut the bonds that hold participants in the Lower Worlds, so they can continue the process of unfoldment in the true Worlds of God.

Initiations bring greater insights into daily living

Initiations unlock souls' Inner awareness, stimulate long-forgotten lessons and rekindle understanding gained in past lives. Each initiation uncovers hidden engrams and life codes that are waiting to be activated and applied to daily living. Each soul is a "walking historical document" existing in a finished creation from the Sugmad's imagination. All knowledge and wisdom is within waiting to be released, but this release must be done in carefully measured increments so that the soul can handle it. Each initiation is the method by which souls reclaim their true heritage as living images of Sugmad and their mastery of the universe in which they live and have their being. Souls are the "prodigal sons" returning home through each initiation to their rightful place as heirs to the Kingdom of Sugmad.

Universal Soul Movement, which is "out of body" projection, is one of the greatest opportunities for the advancement of consciousness in the world today. The initiates in The Way of Truth are universal pioneers who are blazing new trails in hitherto unexplored cosmic territory. The Inner Worlds of God have barely been explored by the average "astral traveler." In most religions, the limits of soul movement have been confined to the Astral Plane. However, there is a vast, unknown frontier waiting to be discovered by humanity. The Way of Truth offers its participants secret roadmaps and guided tours to these mysterious and exciting new worlds.

The one true heart

The true heart of the participant is the essence of who it is as soul. Soul experiences itself directly through the heart center. When soul listens to the subtle messages of its own heart, it is hearing the Voice of God, because this center of its being is designed to be the receptacle of Divine Love. The participants of the Light and Sound of God are taught to develop the qualities of the selfless heart – and this is the "true heart" that beats within the human body.

Unless a heart is selfless, it is of no use to Spirit. The true heart of the participant is the selfless heart that builds the bridge between man's lower ego and his higher, divine self. Only through selflessness can humans cross that bridge to follow their destiny into the True Worlds of God.

The heart governs the mind

Mankind's mental abilities are controlled by the mind and ego, which can only go as far as the Mental Plane; mind cannot reach the God Worlds. True wisdom is not gained through the mind, but is understood through the heart. A deeply wise man or woman is one who has learned the value of selfless love. Mental acuity is useful only in the Lower Worlds of cause and effect. The mind is the tool for soul to interact and acquire knowledge in the physical planes. Once soul has dropped the dense lower bodies, it has no further use for its mental functions. The only thing it takes to the Gates of Heaven is what it has learned about how to love. Spirit is only interested in how much a soul has gained in its capacity to give and receive Love.

Understanding Sugmad's will

To understand the will of Sugmad, souls need only to listen to the subtle voices of their own hearts and intuition. When the chatter of the mind has been quieted and the ego has been put to bed, all truth is made available to soul.

The body is also an indicator of "right" or "wrong" information. If it feels right within the solar plexus, which has been referred to as the "gut instinct," you can trust that it is okay to accept the source of what has been transmitted, but, if one were to experience an uncomfortable heaviness or a feeling of sickness in the pit of the stomach, it is safe to assume that what has been conveyed is not of pure origin or intentions.

The will of Sugmad is always concerned with the welfare of every soul in this universe; it is all-inclusive in scope and nature. So, if guidance is received that encompasses the greatest good for all concerned, it is divinely given. If the guidance appears to be mainly of self-serving interests, it is most likely from the mind of the person, or even from a lower astral being who is attempting to influence that person for their own ends or simply to cause mischief. This brings up an interesting subject of "astral possession." For the sake of this discourse I will not go into elaborate detail, but suffice it to say that much of what motivates the actions of humanity is dictated by the thoughts and desires generated by disembodied astral beings who hover over our world looking for weak spots in a person's consciousness through which they can penetrate the thoughts and manipulate the actions of that individual.

The greatest culprits in the creation of these vulnerable "holes" in the human consciousness are pride, ego and vanity. Astral entities appeal to these vices in their victims and once they are allowed entrance, it is hard to shake them off and know or distinguish what thoughts are those of the person and what are from the outside intrusion.

For participants in The Way of Truth, the voice of the One True God rings clearly in their consciousness through devoted study of the teachings of the Living Master and daily application of the spiritual exercises. This divine course of study strengthens the armor of soul and makes it impervious to interference from negative forces. The mind and ego are stilled and an open channel is created through the heart to receive the love, protection and guidance of the Spiritual Masters and the highest understanding of Sugmad's Will.

The exchanges of teachers and other paths of life

There is a Brotherhood amongst Spiritual Teachers that exists in the Inner Worlds of this universe and functions outside the bounds of established spiritual paths and religious organizations. The one supreme goal of this Divine Order of Masters is to lead as many souls as possible back to the Heavenly Worlds from which they came. There is no competition or possessiveness among these Master Teachers of the Inner realms. Their physical counterparts act in accordance with the rules established in this Divine Order millennia ago when the first Masters of the Cloak of Sugmad walked in the light of the God Worlds. There is an unspoken code of conduct in this Order of Beings to help each soul on the path of enlightenment to move forward in every way possible. If an incarnated Master acknowledges that he has taken a member of his flock as far as he can within the boundaries of his teachings, he will approach a Master of higher learning and introduce that soul to that new Master during the dream state. Then that soul will be lead in their Outer life to the teachings of that higher path of learning. This form of graduation will continue until that soul has acquired full emancipation from the Lower Worlds and reaches the shores of Self-Realization, and ultimately the boundless sea of God-Realization.

Past residual fears and past lives

In each incarnation, soul brings baggage from its previous lifetimes. Hidden fears and repressed emotions make up the majority of the unresolved issues soul carries in its emotional body. It acts unconsciously from these fears and chooses to disguise them behind the false security of the mind. The mind was conceived as a tool for soul to interact in the Lower Worlds. It is a machine that is operated by soul – it has no "life" of its own. Mind is like a car that needs a driver to give it motion and direction. However, over the course of man's evolution, the mind has been exalted to the level of equal status with soul. Man identifies himself with his mind and ego; "I think, therefore I am," is the universal mantra of humankind. Most people are living in a world of comfortable familiarity punctuated with daily routines and rituals that provide an anchor to all that feels secure. If they venture away from the dock of that security into unknown territory, the mind quickly pulls them back to the harbor where it tells them, "Here, you are safe."

Any place the mind cannot fathom is perceived to be "dangerous." As soul advances, the mind is wringing its hands like a worrisome mother hen squawking, "You don't want to go there – you will get hurt!" Over time this builds a sense of fear that lodges in the emotional body, and when a new concept is presented to the consciousness, it retreats to the safety of the mind.

The participants in The Way of Truth have a way out of the controlled environment dominated by the mind; by daily focusing inward on the doorway at the Third Eye, and chanting the holy words of God as given by the Living Master, they are provided with a glimpse of the timeless, spaceless worlds beyond thought and emotion. This is where soul meets itself as a living reflection of All That Is. This is where there is no need to hide and nothing to fear; there is only **SEEING, KNOWING, and BEING.** When soul understands that it is not its mental functions, the bonds of old fears begin to slip away and soul is once again captain of its own destiny, sailing away from the safe shores of average human existence into the oceanic splendors of spiritual truths and divine destinations that await further exploration.

Love multiplies itself like a domino effect

One should always be in a state of preparedness. Those who are prepared to face life's challenges through daily study of their spiritual discourses and practice of the exercises are arming themselves with the best possible defense, protection, wisdom, and guidance as they meet the dawn of each new day. The complacent man is the beaten man – there is no bread on his table, no fire in the hearth, no friends to uplift him, and no God to give his life meaning. This is a world of cause and effect where a sincere effort in the right direction pays great dividends.

Always have a goal before you! Make that goal something that will further your understanding of how to love and be of service to those who struggle along their way. It can be as simple as giving a smile to a tired stranger or a word of encouragement. They will find rest and rejuvenation in the kindness shining in your eyes. This in turn will uplift and recharge the batteries of your own internal engine. Nothing can be given that will not return to the sender – make your contributions with the conscious desire to be of service. This is the High Road to God. Simple kindnesses performed each day are the building blocks of spiritual strength and moral stamina which will come to your aid to handle whatever challenges arise in your life.

God loves those who give love without any though of receiving in return - this is the divine circuit of existence that perpetuates itself with each act of selflessness. Good works are the foundation of man's survival in the physical world – not money or social status or a lovely home with three cars in the driveway. Those are all delicious icings on the cake, but the dough and yeast of love and kindness are what gives that cake substance and form. Do your best to see the good in all people in every circumstance. Be the light that dispels darkness and despair. There is so much suffering in the Lower Worlds, yet there are golden opportunities rising with each morning sun to make someone's burden lighter – not to take the burden upon yourself, but to transform it with an act of love. Be conscious of the world around you – be awake among those who sleepwalk in darkness. Gently guide them back to wakefulness by sharing something you have learned that will open their eyes to the love around and in them. Be an emissary of that love through your own example of cheerfulness and compassion. In this way you will transform your life and everything around you will reflect more beauty, joy and abundance. There will still be challenges to face, but the sun and wind will be always at your back, while the rain clouds will pass quickly far overheard and disappear like mist beyond the horizon. Go forward in confidence knowing that the Masters of the Grand Council and the Sehaji Order walk closely by your side.

The far-reaching vision of the Grand Council and Africa's role

Ours is a very ancient order of Masters; we have seen many universes come and go. Each universe has a preordained destiny and each was created to bring as many souls as possible back to the arms of the Beloved One. There is a multiplicity of evolutions occurring simultaneously within each universal structure in the cosmos. Each one is graduating a "class" of souls who have mastered the Lower Worlds and are ready to take their place among the spiritual hierarchies. This is the goal of every universe in creation – to nurture, train, educate and prepare souls to become one with the will of their Father in the worlds of Heaven. There is no other reason for these universes to exist but to be the places of highest learning and achievement for soul. It is vitally important for each universe to stay in balance between light and dark forces. These are worlds of polarity, as that is how soul learns to understand itself through the opposite poles of awareness; we are all familiar with those polarities of love and hate; light and dark; up and down; left and right; etc. Soul cannot understand a quality without experiencing its opposite. Thus, everything literally hangs in the balance when it comes to successfully completing a cycle of evolution producing a new crop of graduates into the God Worlds.

This universe that we presently inhabit has fallen dangerously out of balance and harmony with the will of Sugmad, and so It has approached the Grand Council of Masters to set things right again. Our vision at present is to create a unified force of spiritual soldiers who will literally go to war with the dark forces. We are arming them with the spiritual artillery they need to win this war. This is where Africa comes in.

Every nation of people needs a form of government where the leadership is headquartered and laws are created to maintain peace and order. It is the leadership that brings lawfulness and balance to the land. We have chosen Africa as the central point of power on Earth where the leadership of the spiritual hierarchies can gather their forces in one united front at one point on the globe. This becomes the catalyst for the powers of good to gain in strength and momentum to overthrow the powers of evil that have long held Earth in its grasp. Our Living Master, Dan Rin, has been assigned to clean up the vibrations of our universal headquarters, our beloved mother Africa, by ridding it of the stranglehold of black magic that has gripped that continent for centuries. So far, he has made great progress in purifying and cleansing the grounds for this holy mission. The process is nearly complete; all that remains is for our warriors of the Light and Sound to advance sufficiently in their training to be to push the scales back in the direction of all that is good in this world – love, courage, kindness, generosity and compassion. All it takes is daily practice of the spiritual exercises as given in the Way of Truth discourses, which are designed to open the heart to be a clear receiver and transmitter of divine love. Our vision is for each and every soul to reclaim their true heritage as sons and daughters of God and to move together, linked in the arms of brotherhood and sisterhood, to bring this universe to the successful completion of its glorious evolution.

Choose love above all things

Love is the center of the universe and the source from which all things flow that have life and destiny. There is no life and there is no destiny without love; by destiny we mean souls returning to their true home in the Sea of Love and Mercy as fully realized God-conscious beings. All other pursuits are secondary to love; even that of wisdom, for there is no wisdom without love. Wisdom without love is only knowledge and knowledge cannot stand the test of time; it flows and ebbs with human consciousness, which is always in a state of flux. Wisdom is eternal and its heart is love. It is the wise soul who chooses love over the transitory goals of common human ambitions in this world such as the attainment of wealth, power and fame. All of that will disappear like a castle made of sand when the high tides of fate wash over the beach, and one must begin building anew. Love is beyond the reach of the vicissitudes of this life; it is the one thing you can always count on to be there. Love does not wither and die; it does not grow old; it cannot go bankrupt; it cannot be stolen from your pocket. True, divine love brings you all the desires of your heart if you seek it for its own sake. Let there be no "ulterior motives" in the pursuit of real love. Give love with no thought of return; just give of yourself wherever you find a need that fits your unique talents and abilities. Be cheerful and a light unto others who struggle in the grip of darkness. This is part of the divinity of love. Then, when you have given selflessly, all of life opens up to you and the riches of soul come pouring in like falling rain.

Love is the highest frequency of Creation in this universe

Love is the Key to All Life in All Universes in All of Eternity. It holds all worlds together and without it, everything would fall into destruction and be made void. Its frequency must supersede every other in creation because all of life moves in the direction of love. Its voice must ring out high and clear above the din of the Lower Worlds to lead all souls back to Its divine sound current, which is the voice of Sugmad Itself.

A contemplative exercise to open the door to a greater conscious state of soul movement

1. Sit comfortably and take several deep breaths until you feel relaxed. Sing HU five times.

2. Imagine you are standing on a bluff over a calm, blue sea with soft white clouds that are tinged with the colors of dawn. It is early morning.

3. Take into your lungs the freshness of the new day and look across the great expanse of moving, living waters. These are the waters of soul. There are no

boundaries, no land anywhere. It is all the living, breathing sea of your consciousness. Enjoy the sense of freedom for a few minutes. Now prepare to dive into that sea.

4. Say the mantra: **"SU-LI-PRANA-O-TE"** (pronounced "soo lee prahnah oh tay") three times very slowly. Now dive from the bluff into the great expanse of your consciousness and immerse yourself in the waves of awareness that catch you and lift you and hold you like a floating ball of light. Simply allow yourself to float and move with the waves of your beingness. Feel that you are expanding into this ocean of oneness with your true self. Everything seems sharper and clearer; sounds are more musical, colors are more brilliant. The sun's warmth on your body soothes your senses as gentle breezes open your consciousness to more feeling and receptivity. Stay in this heightened state of awareness for the next 20 minutes. Allow whatever comes through to play on the screen of your Third Eye. You may also ask a question about anything in your life.

5. Then continue to float peacefully on the gentle waters and listen to the inner depths of your heart as it speaks to you. Blessed be.

(See next page for another contemplative exercise.)

]A contemplative exercise to heighten the vibration of love in the home environment, at work, and at places of recreation.

I would like to try something different with this exercise.

1. Instead of the usual sitting and relaxing and singing of HU, I would like the participant to pick up one of the books or discourses of the Way of Truth, it can be any one, and open to a page at random.

2. Then focus on a line from that page, and read it silently or aloud to yourself. That will be the opening to this exercise. If this is a guided exercise, the facilitator will select the literature and read the opening line aloud to the participants.

3. Now imagine that you are sitting on a giant Ferris wheel, like the kind at an amusement park. Imagine you are at the top of the wheel with a view of the city you live in. You can see in all directions at once from your lofty vantage point. You can see your home, your work, and all your favorite places of recreation from here.

4. As you sit at atop the wheel, imagine invisible arms of light reaching out from your body and stretching over the entire city. Your arms encircle the places of your daily life. Simply imagine embracing them all at once like a mother holding her children close. As you do so, say this mantra three times: **"O-VA-MA-SU-LA-TE"** (pronounced "oh vah mah soo lah tay.")

5. Let the light of your spiritual embrace touch each place in your life – your home, work, etc. Take a moment to inwardly visit each place and say each time, "I bless this environment with love."

6. Then stay in contemplation for the next 15 minutes enjoying the view at the top of your world. Blessed be.

~ ♥ ~

Paramitas, the Gathering of Many Rivers

~ Chapter Two ~

The Five Spiritual Keys

~ ♥ ~

To reach the great Silent Unknown is the hidden and forbidden wish of every aspirant on the trail who seeks to find the fathomless treasures of this universe.

~ ♥ ~

The five spiritual keys of wisdom

The five keys of wisdom a participant must have to gain a foothold into the true worlds of God are: (1) **Love**- being able to distinguish the love which is divine from that of personal affection. It will come down to the individual to decide if they are being motivated by Sugmad's Will or their own. (2) **Service**-this can be a divine calling, as in giving your time to the spreading of The Way of Truth's works in accordance with your own individual creativity and choice, but it is also serving your family and the raising of your children. Your heart must lead you in this second key. (3) **Surrender**- letting go of all attachments and the grip of ego. We are releasing the spiritual tension behind our actions and we are acting in the interests of all concerned. (4) **Faith**- the development of the open heart. It is the building of one's stamina to face our daily challenges; it is a knowingness that Sugmad loves us no matter what errors or grievous mistakes we make. (5) **Honor-** performing our daily tasks and duties with trust, loyalty and devotion. This is what America's young people are doing in Iraq, serving in the United States military in our attempt to put to rest a 2,000 year cycle among Judaic, Christian and Islamic Cultures.

Love, the first spiritual key of wisdom

Love is the first spiritual key of wisdom, because there is no wisdom without love. Everything in life moves in the direction of love; it is the reason we are here. We gather experiences in our quest for love, and through these experiences we grow in spirit and garner the fruits of wisdom.

In a Universal Soul Movement (USM) journey, Milarepa wanted to tell me the story about a US soldier whom we will call Marcus, who fought in the battle at Wounded Knee in December, 1890. Marcus was also a veteran of several Indian campaigns in the West. He was no stranger to the traditions of the Indian tribes. He had compassion for the Lakota Sioux, who lost their heritage, culture and livelihood when the US government took over their lands in South Dakota and they were forced onto reservations where the semi-arid land and poor weather caused low agricultural production. The Indian agents had their food rations reduced to a bare minimum and the Sioux Nation was facing extinction from sickness, starvation and spiritual depravation. They were deprived of hunting the buffalo freely in the prairie and could no longer worship The Great Father in the ways of their ancestors. The traditional ways of a once proud nation were being systematically destroyed by manifest destiny and western expansionism.

The US government grew impatient with the "lazy Indians" who produced no crops, so rations to the Indians were further reduced. The Sioux reinitiated the practice of the Ghost Dance, which was a spiritual practice against the bullets of the blue-coats. The Ghost Dance was perceived by the military as an informal act of war against white peoples. There was already much unrest brewing between the two sides and eventually an altercation ensued, which became known as The Battle at Wounded Knee Creek or The Wounded Knee Massacre. The soldier, Marcus, sacrificed himself to save a Lakota mother and her two children from being killed by weapons fired into the Sioux camp when the fighting began. He performed the supreme act of love when he gave up his life to save these three people who were strangers to him. He had witnessed the wrongs inflicted on the heart of the Native American people and was outraged at the injustices perpetrated against them. And so, he saw his opportunity to "right a wrong" and saved the mother and her children from gunfire by covering them with his own body. At the end of the battle, nearly 300 Lakota men, women, and children had been killed, but these three lives had been spared because of one person's act of selfless love, compassion and heroism.

Service, the second spiritual key of wisdom

The kind of service a soul renders while encased in a physical shell is what determines the direction that soul will take once it enters the God Worlds. The highest form of service one can perform in the Lower Worlds is to give another living soul the ladder and the torch that will guide him or her out of the pit of ignorance and into the light of Self-Realization. This type of service can take many forms - from education and the arts, to science and medicine, to religion and spiritual studies, to business and entertainment, and so forth. Within every human occupation on this earth, no matter how humble, there is the golden seed of opportunity to serve and uplift the hearts of others. And that is where we come to our story.

There was once a boy who lived in the ancient region known as Mesopotamia. He was a simple servant working in the home of a high government official. The boy's name was Lucien. One of Lucien's duties was to bring water from the well in the courtyard for use within the household. One day the boy noticed a crack in the well and reported it to the head servant. A worker was brought in to mend the crack, but as he was working he lost his footing, toppled into the well, and lay injured at the bottom. The boy took it upon himself to rescue the fallen man and hoisted himself down with a rope. It was dark, dank, and the water was very cold. One of the man's legs was broken and the boy tried to carry him on his back but it was no use. During these efforts, the rope gave out and they were both left stranded. They called out for help but nobody heard. A few hours later the sun had vanished from the sky along with the morale of the two souls at the bottom of the well. The worker was an older man with a wife and children who would worry over his absence. He berated Lucien for attempting to rescue him alone rather than alert the household of the accident. Instead of feeling offended by the angry remarks, Lucien took hold of the man's hands and looked into his eyes in that gloomy, dismal place. He said, "When you have fallen as low as you can go and darkness holds you in its grasp, you must look up to the moon and stars that shine in the wake of the departed sun. There is always light to guide you until the sun returns from its slumber and the sky is once again revealed in the dawn of a new day." As he spoke, a luminous moon appeared like a loving eye focused directly into the well. Lucien gently squeezed the man's hands and said, "They will soon come for us, my friend." The man was comforted and his heart was greatly uplifted. Awhile later they heard voices and footsteps approaching and a brilliant light shone into the well. Lucien and the man looked up to see a face outlined by the glow of a blazing torch. A ladder was lowered into the well and the two men were released from their dark prison and lifted into the embracing light of the rising moon and stars.

Surrender, the third spiritual key of wisdom

Oh, sweet surrender, as gentle as the dust on a butterfly's wing, yet strong as the granite on a mountain's face! The wheels of life turn on acts of surrender which allow the flow of Spirit to open and move all things forward. Holding on to anything causes an Inner and Outer stagnation in the unfoldment of soul. Souls cannot move forward when the ropes of attachment bind their movements - any more than a person can move who is tied to a chair. Yes, the chair could be shuffled along, but only very slowly and tediously. Why be attached to anything in this ephemeral, transitory world?

Look at the fires that have destroyed so much land and property in California - here one day and completely gone the next. Material attachment is the number one hindrance to reaching the magnificent freedom of the God Worlds. Emotional attachment is a close second in this race to non-freedom. Holding on to the past is a lost cause because there is only the Eternal Now beating in the heart of every soul on Earth. The purpose of memories is to teach souls to learn from their past experiences; they are not meant to torment or keep souls bound to a past that has already been played out. *"Do not take back what has already been resolved."*

True surrender is the key to the sacred teachings of the Ancient Ones who once walked the earth before time was born. Only a heart truly free and detached from worldly desires can bathe in the rivers that flow in torrents from their oceans of divine wisdom, knowledge, and understanding. A truly wise soul is one whose heart has no bindings to the illusory School of Maya.

Take this Inner test to see where you stand in the freedom of soul. Just how detached are you right now? Think of someone you love deeply and ask yourself if you would be okay if they were to leave your life to pursue a personal or spiritual goal that would require them to move on in order to grow and make that goal a reality. Could you stand back and allow them to go? Could you sincerely wish them well? Or would the ropes from your emotional body attempt to keep them bound to you through guilt and obligation? Any answer is all right, you are not being judged; it is simply for you to have an honest assessment of where you are in the ability to surrender. When you release a thing freely, it has the choice to return to you, but strangling it with ropes gives it nowhere to go and all would fall into stagnation.

Surrender is also an aspect of the Law of Silence; it is knowing how much or how little to say, or when to say nothing at all. To remain silent when the mind wants to speak its judgments and unsolicited opinions is a supreme act of surrender. True surrender is letting go of the need to control a person or situation. For instance, we can give a friend neutral advice when they ask for it, but if they are about to do something we believe to be a big mistake, and they do not ask for our help, we must stand back and let them have their own experience. That is the way soul learns and grows, and you will grow as well from the practice of discretion and restraint, which equals silence, surrender, and true wisdom.

Wisdom is an ocean of ever-increasing waves of awareness and perception in the development of soul, and surrender is the key which allows that awareness to move freely in search of its highest spiritual potential.

Faith, the fourth spiritual key of wisdom

Let's begin with this question – what do we mean by "faith"? Is it faith in God, in ourselves, or in the material or spiritual worlds? There are all kinds of faith, but only one kind that will get us into the God Worlds and that is faith in **love**. How do we have faith in love? First, we have to act from the belief that we are loved; we are created from and have our being in love, and that is the foundation of our unique faith.

Faith is the engine that gives souls their forward movement and love is the fuel. Faith in love is what we are referring to as one of the spiritual keys of wisdom. What would be an example of this kind of faith? To know that there is nothing in this universe that exists outside of love – no matter what it looks like on the outside, it is all love within. Faith is trust and belief in that love and its attributes include determination, steadfastness, resolve, and commitment.

Wise souls see the opportunity to learn about love in every situation they encounter, and no matter how dire a condition may be, there is a lesson to learn about love, and faith is what motivates them to discover that valuable lesson. When disaster strikes the human experience, the true light of soul is revealed; tests of faith in love abound. Here follows the story of Mictetus who lived in the ancient Roman city of Pompeii at the time of the great volcanic eruption of Mt. Vesuvius in 79 AD.

Mictetus was a slave of the imperial order whose duty it was to serve a general under the rule of Emperor Augustus. He worked to his highest ability to please the general in order to eventually earn his freedom. Many slaves in those days went on to become successful private citizens with their own businesses and homes. This is what Mictetus aspired to in his servitude to General Cornelius and his family. He felt no real affection for his employer, as he was forced into slavery at an early age and simply worked to earn his freedom. Yet Mictetus had a good heart and could be counted on to be loyal and trustworthy. Cornelius recognized this in him and secretly vowed to keep him as his most valued slave, although outwardly he gave the promise that Mictetus would one day be a free man. Mictetus had faith that his master would eventually grant his release from slavery and even employ him in the imperial army, as this was what the general had implied. So the servant spent his days working very hard to please his master and dreamed of his life as a free agent.

One day the general was visited by a colleague and Mictetus came to serve them a very lavish meal. He left the room, but then realized he had not poured the wine, and turned to come back. That is when he overheard the visitor tell the general what a good servant he had in Mictetus. "Yes," said the general, "and I will never part with him, he is my most valued slave." All of Mictetus' hopes came crashing down around him like an avalanche of broken dreams. He felt betrayed by his master. He said nothing but wondered what to do. His thoughts ran to vengeance, and he knew a lot of Cornelius's personal secrets. "I can drive you into the ground," he thought from the depths of his pain. Cornelius was a respected citizen of Pompeii with a wife and daughter, and had much to lose if his secrets were revealed. This all played through Mictetus' mind as he pondered his future actions, but in his heart of hearts, he knew he could not betray his master that way; it was not in his nature to do so. He still had faith that his master would do the right thing one day and set him free.

It was now late summer, and there had been much rumbling coming from the local volcano of Mt. Vesuvius. The citizens of Pompeii paid little attention while the ground shook from this rumbling, as they were quite used to it, but one day the rumbling became quite loud and ominous clouds of thick ash bellowed out of the volcano's mouth. Around noon, a 12-mile high cloud of ash and rock spewed into the air and blotted out the sun. Suddenly there was panic in the city as people ran out of their homes and into the streets. Some ran to the beach where they thought they would be safer than in the city. At the home of General Cornelius there was a heavy sense of dread. He ordered everyone into the wine cellar under the house; Mictetus was among them. As the molten rock from Vesuvius continued to pour from its mouth, the air in the city became darker and denser with ash. Mictetus thought, "We cannot stay here, we will be suffocated." He urged the general to leave the house and seek a safer place. The general was stubborn, but the looks of terror on the faces of his family convinced him that perhaps his slave was right, so they left their villa and set off into the streets. They were nearly trampled by running people and wild horses.

Mictetus knew of a cave deep within the earth that could offer them shelter; it was often used by slaves who wanted to get away from their owners. It led to the other side of the city and offered an escape route from the main devastation of the volcanic eruption. So, he guided the Cornelius family and held the daughter close, as light was now obliterated and they made their way blindly. Without Mictetus to guide them they would surely have fallen into danger. In fact, he had had a fleeting thought of leaving Cornelius and his family to die so that he could gain his freedom, but in his heart he knew he had to help them. He had a strong faith in the ultimate goodness in men, and in the love in their hearts. This faith is what drove him to protect and help the man who would have kept him a slave. Were it not for Mictetus' great inner faith in love, the Cornelius family would have perished, but this man, Mictetus, who was a captive on earth was free as soul, with a faith greater than the volcano that tried to swallow his entire world. He led his master's family to safety and they were among the few to survive that volcanic eruption that took the lives of so many others. His great faith in love saved four lives, including his own, and won him his freedom on earth and in Spirit. Mictetus kept his faith and found his freedom.

Honor, the fifth spiritual key of wisdom

First, let's discuss what we mean by honor as a key to wisdom. To be honorable is to be forthright with one's dealings with others; this calls for fairness and honesty. Honor is trustworthiness and the ability to maintain silence and secrecy when called for. One of the main requirements of honor is a selflessness of spirit. Honoring others is to put their needs ahead of our own. Yes, we must always look out for our own welfare and survival, but in situations of war and other man-made or natural disasters, we must be willing to come to the aid of our fellow man. To stand with honor is to stand head and shoulders above the average state of consciousness. Being honorable also means demonstrating bravery in the face of very great danger; it is much easier to flee when the bullets are flying and the cannons are blasting than it is to stay and fight and protect what we love and hold most dear. Here follows the story of Caleb, a Union soldier who fought in the Civil War between the North and South of the United States in 1863.

Caleb was the younger of two brothers; the older one was named Christopher. They both served under Grant's armies in the Union forces. There had always been much rivalry between the two brothers, especially in regard to women. Caleb was very jealous of Christopher's fiancée, who had initially been Caleb's sweetheart, but was lured away by the charms and promises of his handsome older sibling. Caleb believed that his brother had no intentions of keeping his romantic promises to the pretty young woman; he just wanted another conquest in the ongoing rivalry with his younger brother. One day Caleb accosted his brother and angrily demanded of him, "Where is your sense of honor?" A fight between the two brothers quickly ignited and both were left with the visible results of their heated animosity on their faces and bodies.

Meantime, there was a much more serious war going on outside of the two bickering brothers. General Meade was leading the Army of the Potomac into Pennsylvania for what was later to be known as the most decisive and pivotal of the Civil War battles – the Battle of Gettysburg. Caleb and Christopher served in the same cavalry as a lieutenant and major, respectively. Their time of reckoning came on the battleground between Little Round Top and Cemetery Hill when the Confederate forces under General Lee were gaining in fierce determination and "pulling out all the stops." The ensuing battles cost the lives of thousands of men on both sides. Though Caleb resented what he perceived as his brother's lack of discretion when it came to affairs of the heart, he did still recognize the outstanding qualities of courage and perseverance his older brother demonstrated on the battlefield. Christopher was a front lines kind of soldier who did not shrink from the sound of cannon blasts over his head. He saved many of the lives of his companions with skilled and brave fighting maneuvers. So, when a bullet tore into his shoulder and knocked him off his feet, his brother Caleb ran from cover out into the open to help him. "Go, Brother," implored Christopher to the younger man. "There is gunfire everywhere – you'll get hurt!" But Caleb stayed and hoisted his brother up and carried him away from the chaos, narrowly missing being hit from all sides as gunfire and the smell of sulfur permeated the earth and sky.

Once he'd gotten Christopher to a place of safety, Caleb made the decision to run for medical aid. He had to cross an open firing range and his brother cried out to him, but Caleb could not dishonor all that he had learned from his older sibling about valor in time of war. The sweetheart who had left him was a fading memory and he suddenly realized that jealousy had clouded his judgment about Christopher. All that mattered now in Caleb's mind and heart was to save the life of that one brave soldier on the battlefield. He wanted more than anything else to get help to his brother who would die of his wounds without proper treatment. So he ran out and almost made it to the medical tents when a bullet opened his head and he fell onto the bloody grounds of Gettysburg. Caleb was one of about 40,000 dead and wounded that day. His brother, Christopher, survived his wounds and went back home to Virginia to marry his fiancée. They named their first child after the family member who had died for what he loved and held most dear. They vowed that one day their newborn son, Caleb, would hear all about his namesake who placed honor above all else; even before himself.

How the five spiritual keys of wisdom are the cornerstone for entry into all the spiritual cities of the upper and lower universes

Master Leytor:

One cannot gain entry into a field of purity without the pure substance of the keys of love, service, surrender, faith and honor completely molded, honed and shaped to fit the locks of the grand doors to the mysterious worlds of Sugmad. Each virtue must be truly assimilated into the consciousness and mastered. There is no in-between area of development here. Mastery of these five keys is essential for the dissolution of karmic debris found within the lower bodies of soul, and for those lower bodies to be light enough to drop once soul stands at the doorway to the first realm of the true worlds of Spirit. There are many realms to travel in the limitless frontier of Sugmad's consciousness. To cross the threshold from the lower kingdoms into the **pristine** realms of spiritual beingness, one must be skilled in the ability to Love in all its highest aspects, and surrender all lower attachments; no baggage is allowed on your travels to higher realms of existence. If any impurity remains in the heart, all travel is limited to the Fourth Plane; a heart bearing the shadows of selfish pursuits cannot withstand the searing light of truth that creates the doorway to the Silent Unknown. All wisdom is borne in Silence; and there is no silence without the keys to wisdom being fully engrained into the experience of soul. This is just one of many steps it takes to reach even the bottom rungs of the God Worlds. I cannot emphasize enough the need for purity in thought, action, and expression. Where I come from, everything is in a state of supreme receptivity and alertness to ALL THAT IS. There is no such thing as mind, which is an ancient relic of the lower bodies dropped long ago into the raging rivers of Light and Sound which drown the individual ego, and cleanse and tear away all remaining dross from soul, leaving it open and raw to its true nature as a child of God and Spirit.

To reach the great Silent Unknown is the hidden and forbidden wish of every aspirant on the trail who seeks to find the fathomless treasures of this universe. I say "hidden" because no one who talks about it to others can reach this destination. This is a pursuit in solitude with only the Master's light to guide you. And I say "forbidden" because it is not granted to those who would trample the gates in their haste for entrance into the Holy of Holies. Those who desire instant gratification of the senses, let them go to an amusement park. What I am speaking of here is for the serious student to leave their personality behind and take up the hem of the mantle of wisdom. What cloak do you follow as you move through the days of your life? First you must identify what it is that motivates and spurs you to activity, what burns in your consciousness that must be pursued? If it is anything to do with a material goal of wealth or other worldly quests, then you are not ready for this Path. This road is for the one who humbly stands naked at the hem of the Master's Cloak; who dons the robe of obedience and silent observance as he or she follows the Master's footsteps. If you are interested only in social acceptance and happy banter with your comrades, you will fade from this road like the last rays of sun on the brink of evening. This is the path of self-surrender and inner trust and silence. No one will pat you on the back and let you know how you are progressing. You will know yourself when you sense that your heart feels lighter, and the awareness of your closeness to God settles on you like a warm and gentle mist.

Here follows a spiritual exercise on how to access your Inner keys of wisdom

1. Imagine five golden keys in your Inner vision, each one sitting in the lock of a separate door. You have only to turn the key to open that particular door. Each door represents one of the spiritual virtues of wisdom: Love, Service, Surrender, Faith, and Honor.

2. Go to the first door of Love and say this mantra: **"AH-SE-TU-BA-FLO-RE-SET,"** Then turn the key, open the door, and step across the threshold. What is the first thing you see as you step through the doorway? What is waiting on the other side? Write down whatever images or feelings come to you.

3. Then do the same thing with the other four keys and use the same mantra each time. This will bring into your daily awareness the flow and creativity of the spiritual keys of wisdom that are already part of your higher consciousness. Blessed be.

How these spiritual keys prepare the God seeker for Universal Soul Movement (USM)

Again, there can be no substantial forward soul movement unless there is absolute purity of consciousness. One way to develop this level of purity is through the constant and focused application of acts of love, service, surrender, faith and honor. There are no shortcuts on the road to spiritual freedom; a lazy man will not see the Face of God. However, this is not like a Dickensian sentence of steel gray servitude and mirthless study. There is great joy in all the virtues that the Sugmad has bestowed upon soul; and the greatest joy is in living those virtues and sharing the fruits of that life experience with others. Soul movement is all about life and giving. There is nothing static in the mercy of God's love for soul; it is always in a state of flux and movement. The endless pool of love within and without soul is always seeking more of Itself. There is no great secret to USM; it is all about staying in the flow of the love and wisdom from your own heart. The spiritual exercises as taught by Dan Rin will facilitate your own natural ability to swim in the Sea of Love and Mercy with a direction and purpose that you as soul were endowed with by the One who awaits your return to the golden fields of Pure Beingness. Words cannot fully express all I have to say on this subject, but I hope to have left you with the "feeling" of the truth in these humble sentences, for I am your humble servant, invited here at the graceful invitation of the Living Master to shed a ray of light and hope for all who travel the roads to spiritual emancipation. Your sincere desire to seek God, light, truth, love, joy and wisdom is your real and first key to unlocking the mysteries within your own heart, spirit, and destiny. This is the launching pad of USM.

Here is a second exercise on how to weigh the spiritual wisdom of choices we must make for our lives

1. Imagine that you are sitting in a classroom and there is a large blackboard at the front of the room. Whenever there is a choice to make in your daily life, see yourself going to that Inner blackboard and writing down the question of the choice you face.

2. Then take an imaginary eraser and wipe out the question. Close your Inner eyes and say this mantra: **"VO-LE-TU-SO-MA-TE"** (pronounced "voh lay too soh mah tay.") Say it three times.

3. Then open your eyes and look for the answer to your question. If it is not immediately visible on the blackboard, say, "Thank you for the wisdom of my choice," and go on with your day. The right and wisest choice will thereafter be impressed upon your consciousness and you will simply KNOW what to do. Blessed be to all sincere travelers of the Light and Sound.

~ Chapter Three ~

The Silent Journey Within

~ ♥ ~

*Only in silence can true wisdom enter the House of Soul, and only in wisdom can true love make that dwelling a **home** that is strong enough to withstand all the elements of destruction that would tear it to the ground.*

~ ♥ ~

The great silent unknown

The great silent unknown is the unexplored vast and hidden heart of soul and its true and mysterious essence exists as a being of God. This is not "soul searching" or meditation or religious study or kneeling in prayer. It cannot be found in any books in any worlds or in any universes. It has no language or external points of reference and it cannot be encompassed by the mind. It can be found in the breath of expectation when the sun climbs over the horizon; and **it is the breath within that breath.** The great silent unknown lives in between conscious spaces of reality. It is the shadow behind the face of the moon, and then the shadow within that shadow. It is the song of the stars, and then the song within that song. And still, it is there but not there, because it is always moving beyond the rim of ordinary consciousness. It is a super-conscious state of non-beingness. When you are "aware" of anything, it takes on the form of your individual conscious awareness, and so it becomes a non-silence, because silence has nothing to do with individual consciousness; it has to do with a state of waiting receptivity, of no movement toward anything. Instead, you allow the thing to come to you as it will in its pure and unblemished state. We cannot move into the great silent unknown because it is not a destination. It is the living NO-THING that sustains the life within all life. The mind cannot grasp the concept of true nothingness; it is always in a state of reacting to stimuli. So, to truly step into the first stage of the vast unknown reaches of the mystery of the true self, the mind must be sent away and kept busy like a dog chasing after a stick. Throw the stick as far as you can and have the mind chase it until you are left in the quiet of your heart. That begins the process of finding the breath within the breath until there is no more consciousness of breathing; instead there arises an alertness and receptivity to the silence that waits to reveal itself.

When people are fully engrossed in a task they enjoy, and are no longer conscious of their body or their next breath, they are in that state of alert receptivity that I have referred to above. Allowing in the silence does not mean deadening the senses or sitting like a zombie. It is not holding the breath, hoping for a glimpse of the silent unknown while you are steadily choking. It is more like the Law of Reversed Effort where the least exertion produces the strongest results. Simply see, know and BE. You can even say this to yourself as you sit in contemplation: **"I see, know and become ONE with the Silence within my Self."** Then wait expectantly for the first veil to be lifted and the veil within that one, and so on, until there is nothing between you and the great Inner unknown mystery that is the One and Silent Heart.

The love in silence

There is weakness in too much "talking," both outwardly and inwardly. Runaway thoughts do as much damage as runaway words. Excessive verbal expression creates "leakages" within the consciousness and lower bodies of man. These leaks or openings allow the invasion of outside influences to affect the conduct and productivity, or lack thereof, in a human being. They also allow illness – physical, mental and emotional – into the experience of the lower bodies. This does not mean one should never speak or express oneself; it means to reflect inwardly on each word that comes out of your mouth, mind, and pen. It is more than to ask yourself, "Is it true, necessary, and kind?" It is to **inwardly reflect on the consequences** of what is released to the outside world. Every single word has an Inner point of reference that can create a domino effect as the points connect and release the energy contained within the vibration of that word. These energetic vibrations live for a long time in the ethers surrounding and penetrating this world, and they attract like particles of energy that can maintain life forms of their own that think and act and have their being for a limited time until the energy is dissipated. The Astral Plane is filled with such "thought phantoms" that can create a certain amount of effect, for good or for bad, in the Lower Worlds. The nature of a word determines its "appearance" as a thought in the Astral Plane, and the strength and quality of emotion with which it is released determines its personality. Many of these words create the "monsters" we see in our nightmare visions. Others become like guardian angels that hover over an individual in sleep and waking life. So take care what you decide to release into this world of constant creativity because you are one of the architects of this very Universe!

Now, let us look at the relevance and importance of Silence as one of the God seeker's greatest strengths. Silence is the greatest form of creativity in the mysteries of spiritual life. It is the springboard of the conscious forward movement and expression of soul as it launches itself from the heart of God. Only in silence can true wisdom enter the House of Soul, and only in wisdom can true love make that dwelling a **home** that is strong enough to withstand all the elements of destruction that would tear it to the ground. Silence is the rock and mortar of soul's true home in the

Living Word of God. The Word is Silent Agreement with All Life. How does one create with silence? When the mind and ego are stilled, the heart opens to all the possibilities of God's limitless imagination. It is a silent endeavor to imagine anything, and all creation springs from the imagination of man, who is a reflection of the Original Creator. In silence, there is nothing to get in the way of divine creativity; there are no thought forms interfering with true communion with God's love for all of life. Remember that you are children of that one great LOVE, and you can flow into it when you allow silence to be your guide. It is not a hard or unhappy thing to be within the great silent space of your Self, nor is it lonely, because silence opens the door to your true home in the Kingdom of your Father who loves you with deep and unconditional devotion. You do not need the racket of words to find company in this physical world. You need only to stop and listen to receive the unspoken kinship of truth that waits to embrace you in the sweet and sacred silence of joyous, creative Life.

The experience of the "spiritual void" in the God Worlds toward the Twelfth Plane and above

There is a realm at the doorway to higher consciousness that is actually a protective field of suspended energy that divides the higher planes of the purest worlds of God from that of the lower God planes. The energy becomes activated when a soul enters this territory. This is a "no man's land" that all souls must cross before they are allowed access to the gates of Sugmad's innermost kingdoms. No soul can pass through this void without the presence of one of the Masters of the Inner realms. One can try, but there is the strong possibility of becoming "lost" in this void, much like the disappearances within the Bermuda Triangle. It is a safety measure that separates those who are not ready for this sacred journey into the greatest mysteries of Life from those who are developed enough to withstand the intense vibrations of these lofty worlds. You may ask, "What is it like to pass through this void?" It is like being drawn into an immense vacuum with the air violently sucked out of your lungs. In the soul body, you are not subjected to the effects of the physical shell, so there is no suffocation, etc., but you feel as if your very being has been torn from you and shredded in the vast, swirling nothingness of the Void. This is actually a process of purification to dissolve the last remnants of dross still clinging to the magnetic resonance of the soul body. The presence of a spiritual master of great merit insures that this process goes smoothly and without dangerous consequences for the soul. Only one who has traversed this realm many times is qualified to be a guide for those who are attempting to cross the border into the Great Unknown. It is not a journey for the faint of heart, but for the bold and adventurous soul who is ready to take the next gigantic leap forward in development and experience. This is Mastership territory and once entered, there is no turning back to the comfort zones of old ways of living. It is more than an Initiation into Higher Grounds; it is the death of the lower ego forever and the assimilation of consciousness into the ONE great consciousness of God. There is no loss of individuality, but the blending of soul with the Will of Its Father. It is a ride of great courage and joy for those willing to make the commitment, for the rewards are vast and unlimited. There are many Guides ready to take your hand when the time has come for you to make this great journey to the first true worlds of the Spiritual Kingdoms. I will be among those who will welcome you to your new Home in the Heart of Universal Love, Beauty, and Truth. We await your presence!

The "aloneness" experienced by the God seeker in the God Worlds is a positive effect of spiritual growth

One cannot reach the homeland of divine mercy, beauty, love and joy unless they have reached that state of consciousness where they have found the gem of solitude within themselves. This is not a journey to be made in fellowship with others; it is the Journey of the Soul with only the Light of the Masters to guide it. There are many roads to the Sublime and Eternal Realms of God, but all roads come to a point where soul must go the remainder of the journey alone. It has always been that way. The Master will take you just so far, and shines the light of his love and protection before you, and it is that light that will be your companion for the remainder of your trek to higher grounds.

Soul is, in essence, a singular unit of awareness from the living breath of Sugmad. There is no such thing as "twin souls" or even "soul mates" **in the fullness of the definition used in modern Metaphysics** because this implies that soul cannot stand by itself without leaning on the experience of another. Soul finds comfort in its friends and family; and in love, passion, and romance with a beloved, but in the end, soul must find its way back to its origins alone. Aloneness is a thing of sacred beauty because only in solitude does soul hear the voices of Eternity calling to it and advising it of its true nature. Only in the secret chamber of the quiet self does one truly commune with God. Sometimes a life requires that relationships fall away so that the soul can take the next steps that would otherwise be hidden from view by the influence of too many people who would hold it back. This has often happened with the Living Masters; in that a very few people could remain as comrades due to the difficulty of the road they have chosen to follow, but it is a road of immense beauty and joy once the rocks and thorns of the lower ego have been dissolved and crushed by determination and courage.

If you are a sincere seeker of God, and find yourself alone with no one to talk to who truly understands you, this is a sign of spiritual growth, because the higher you go in consciousness, the fewer people there will be who can keep up the pace and walk by your side. Most will begin to fall behind and then simply disappear from your life. This is natural and necessary because when soul reaches a certain point in its development, there can be fear and jealousy sent from those with whom soul had close relationships; and those negative feelings will attempt to interfere with that soul's forward movement. So Spirit creates natural barriers around that person who is ready to take the first serious steps away from all that they have known and guides them to the doorway of the true mysteries of higher knowledge and wisdom. It is a very lonely path, but the rewards are so great as to make any personal sacrifices seem trifling by comparison. And this is not to sound cold-hearted, because for those close ones who can give that soul their unconditional love and support, there will always be the bond of affection to connect them in the heart of eternity; they will never be lost to each other.

Aloneness is a great virtue to be cultivated in the heart of all sincere seekers of the highest realms of God consciousness. It is what separates the wheat from the chaff as the One Father harvests Its own from the fields of the Lower Worlds and takes them back to the Homelands of Eternal Love and Mercy.

Herein follows an uplifting contemplative prayer for all God seekers

The Prayer of the Lighted Heart

Deep within the heart of man
Is a candle waiting to be lighted
By the oil of love and devotion
And the flame of forgiveness and freedom

For your candle to burn brightly,
You must go within the holy cathedral of yourself
And enter the silent chamber of your own confessional
Where God is the receiver of your secret truths

God will bear witness to the suffering
You have borne within yourself and caused to others.
Once the last word of your confession has been uttered
A lightness of spirit will prevail and
All darkness shall be banished.

The Silent Journey Within

Now stillness will come over you that is like the pristine air
Of the dawn just visible as a mist on the far horizon
And in which all things are possible
In the gentle solitude of the newly risen day.

In this solitude of the unburdened heart
You will find that place within yourself
Where the candle of soul awaits the fire of Self-Realization
To become the light of a thousand flames

Each divine spark of your awareness
Lights the candles of hope and desire
In the hearts of those who seek redemption and healing
From the One who bears all suffering.

To kneel at the divine altar of love and mercy
Is to free yourself from the grasp of darkness
And as you stand to raise your candle
To the fire of the Sacred Heart within

A thousand other candles rise into the air
Until there is a blaze of light so brilliant
Not one heart remains in shadows,
Not one soul stands alone

But all are illuminated and united
By the purifying fires of tolerance,
Forgiveness, hope and grace,
That burn in the heart of the Giver of all Light and Salvation.

~Blessed Be~

Maintaining full consciousness of the God State moment-by-moment while in the Awake State

Master Leytor:

It is a simple thing to maintain this high state of awareness and that is the first understanding one must have before going into contemplation; because as soon as you decide it is difficult to do, the mind will step in and insure that progress will be hindered. So let's decide right now that it is easy and joyful to get into the God State! There are many methods of preparing the consciousness for the journey into the higher realms of awareness that have already been discussed in your discourses, such as chanting HU or your personal word, or other names of God that open the heart to Love. Simply use one of those spiritual tools as taught by the Living Master and allow yourself to fly like a bird into the sky of your imagination, because imagination is the key to unlocking your ability to maintain the God State of awareness! This is the priceless gift that the Creator has bestowed upon his children, and so all that is necessary to "take flight" is to use a word of high vibratory essence that will launch you from the mundane physical world and then use your divine creativity to imagine where you want to go and who you wish to see. Let the journey unfold as it will; go along for the ride and enjoy the sights, sounds, feelings, and imagery that open to your Inner vision and senses. This is like going to the movies of soul; enjoy the experience as one who not only observes from a "safe" distance, but also gets involved as a creator and participant in the action!

To maintain this higher state of consciousness throughout your day, you have only to use one of the key contemplative words as mentioned above; and simply chant it inwardly to yourself whenever you think about it. It would be good to sing your Word, or HU, or another word of spiritual merit every hour or two. This will keep the Inner vibratory signature strong with the message of soul and it will permeate all that you encounter in your daily life, and raise it to the highest level possible. You will attract the highest possible outcomes in your daily challenges and also bring out the highest aspects of consciousness in those people who come into your rate of vibration. A great place to practice this discipline is in the work environment where you are likely to uplift many people who may be struggling and in need of encouragement. You do not even have to speak to them; they will be uplifted by your very presence when you practice singing the holy words of God to yourself. It is a very simple thing to do with very far reaching results. I am glad to speak on this subject, because it is a part of Best-Laid Plans to balance this universe; it begins with each individual soul, affecting other souls in the most beneficial way for the advancement of all mankind.

Silence develops Universal Soul Movement and Inner dialogue with the Inner Master

Silence is the Master Key that unlocks soul's ability to commune with the Divine. Once the initial spiritual word or words of merit are uttered, one begins to fall into a silence, and it is in this holy space of quietude where the

Inner Master will appear to your waiting heart. You can have discourse with each other on any subject of concern in your life; you may ask any question and find yourself being taken to a place of learning within the Inner Worlds. Once you ask a question from this receptive state of awareness, it is often the catalyst for USM with the Inner Master to one of the Temples of Wisdom in the Worlds of God. You may simply find yourself in a classroom, or in a garden, sitting with a Master who has the expertise to answer your question most fully. Silence allows the smooth transition from the waking state to the contemplative state of moving the soul on an unbounded journey into the realms of true wisdom and learning. The moment that mind begins to question this Inner movement all is stopped and you will return to your physical body. It is only in maintaining the focus on the silence in your heart and allowing what is to simply BE that you will be uplifted into the presence of the Inner Master and be able to hear his words to you and journey with him to the places of mystery where only the power of silence can take you.

How the God State refines the projectory of thoughts and actions

In the human state all actions are the result of thoughts projected from the mind and ego. In the God State one acts from the center of love in the heart region. This is a tremendous leap in consciousness. In the God State of awareness the mind is shut off completely and soul is motivated by the highest virtues of love, compassion, kindness and mercy. Everything soul does in this state is for the greater good and takes the individual out of the limited consciousness of "me" and "mine" and into the expanded realm of "we" and "ours," which is the state of Brotherhood. When soul is cognizant of life outside its own small circle of awareness, the projection of its thoughts and actions reaches far across the universal boundaries of ordinary thought. When thoughts are propelled by the God State, their refinement can penetrate through the grosser thought forms that inhabit the atmosphere and even change their vibratory structure. Thus, the energy of a "heavy thought" of malice is significantly diluted when penetrated by a pure projection of love. The higher the refinement of thought, the greater is its power to weaken and even destroy baser elements created from the mind of humanity. A thought of love can also intercept and change the course of a negative projectile and send it back to its source. Thoughts are like video games in a sense; you can perform "search and destroy" missions with your thoughts by imagining them as blue comets of the Light and Sound going after the red splotches of the Kal forces and blowing them into oblivion!

Any thought of goodness that you project has a positive impact on the environment in which you live. The atmosphere becomes more refined and uplifting and has the ability to influence the consciousness of others in a beneficial way, and even promote physical and emotional healing and well being. When one is uplifted, all are uplifted. We do not walk this journey through the Lower Worlds alone; we take our brothers and sisters with us. Let us always project the highest in what we think and do in our daily lives. We can refine and balance this universe one thought at a time.

Thoughts move back and forth through Time and Space

A thought can be projected back in time or into the future by an act of concentrated will of the sender. One must be fully conscious and focused in this ability and it cannot be used for anything other than goodwill and good intentions. If one wishes to send a thought of harm or destruction to an individual or group of people, this is tantamount to black magic and will reap very severe repercussions for the sender. Unfortunately, most thoughts that hover in the atmosphere were unconsciously created by the wild and untamed tides of human emotions. The stronger the emotion behind the thought, the longer it will live and the farther it will travel. Some thoughts during times of extreme trauma, as during war or natural disaster or personal tragedy, can last for centuries before they are finally dissipated. Some of these thoughts can appear as "ghosts" to those with clairvoyant ability and often are mistaken for real persons because they can take on the appearance of the one who projected the original thought. What we understand as "hauntings" in houses and other structures, are often the phantoms of lingering thoughts created by the former inhabitants of those environments.

As you can see, a thought can be a very powerful energy in these Lower Worlds and can take on a life of its own, and even stay alive for years and centuries. Thoughts that transcend time and space are often those that continue to receive energy from the descendants of the original thought! A thought of grief or revenge, for instance, can live for many years when fed by the minds of the families and friends of a murder victim. This goes out and creates havoc in the sensitive ethers that permeate the environment in which we live on Earth. Have you ever felt a sudden, intense sadness for no reason? This can be the result of "picking up" on the thought form created from a grieving family who suffered a tragedy in the nineteenth century. The examples of living thoughts are endless and the bottom line is that we must be very careful and responsible when projecting our minds and emotions into the world!

There are ways to consciously create and send thoughts of goodwill and healing to affect not only the present, but the past and future as well. One can literally go into the past and change its course with a thought projected from a highly-charged, concentrated and focused act of will. This is a highly refined skill for use only by Initiates of the Ninth Plane and above who are mentored and supervised by one or more of the Sehaji Masters. It is not a skill to be trifled with or used for personal gain or amusement. And it will not be discussed further in this discourse. It is only to illustrate to you, my dear reader, how profound and serious is the nature of the power of our ability to think and create reality from our thoughts. If you do the spiritual exercises as given by the Living Master and strive always to keep your heart open to the purity of divine love and compassion, you will become one of the sacred architects of this universe and a co-worker with the angels and arch-angels who govern the realms of goodness on earth.

Universal Soul Movement can collapse Time and Space

When one has sufficiently learned the art of USM, time and space are no longer relevant because they are part of the illusion of the Lower Worlds. With USM one transcends the physical realms completely because the vision and goal is to move toward the God Worlds. Since there is no physical movement of the lower bodies, there is no element of time or space to contend with. Once a spiritual word of merit, such as HU, has been chanted and the attention placed on the Third Eye, you have only to imagine where you wish to go in your soul travels and that will be enough to get you there. Moving the soul consciousness is instantaneous because imagination and desire are all that is required to make the journey, and so time and space "collapse" as soul leaves the world of cause and effect and moves into the boundless worlds of Spirit.

Another aspect of USM is the ability to "stretch" time and space. This involves the use of specific mantras that open a vortex of energy between the various planes below the Great Divide in which time and space can be manipulated. Days can be made longer or shorter and space can be made to expand or contract. What you experience as time on Earth is merely an agreement you've made with other souls that there are so many minutes in an hour and so many hours in a day. The truth is that there is only an eternal "now" that stretches from one end of the universe to the other. Humanity has broken it down into increments that make sense in the physical world so that it can experience physical reality in a context of social acceptance, but the reality is that no two people experience time in exactly the same way, and what is a short day for one person is a long day for another. So consciousness is another way to manipulate time, and also space.

The Masters who contributed to the creation of this universe have often manipulated time in order to stay in alignment with the plans of this Sugmad to bring this universal creation to its final cycle of completion. As people grow older they often comment that time is moving more rapidly with each passing year. This is not a figment of their imagination but is an actual effect of the acceleration of motion that the Masters of this Universe have created to move things forward in progress. So, you have many different layers of time and space occurring simultaneously in the Lower Worlds. Universal Soul Movement allows you to transcend the effects of the various levels at which we experience physical reality by taking you to the source of creation and existence in the heart of the God Worlds where all time and space collapse into the swirling vortex of true beingness in the infinite state of the Eternal Now.

The God State can facilitate a higher "Art of Manifestation"

Creativity is the source of all reality; it is the divinely bestowed gift from God to Its children, allowing them the ability to create and live in Its image. There are many levels of creative endeavor, from the culinary arts to the literary and fine arts, and so on. This requires a level of expertise and innate talent on the part of the practitioner of these arts that have their being in the physical world. However, there is a higher form of art that has its source in the God Worlds far above the Great Divide, and that is the ability to manifest reality – the Art of Manifestation. This particular, highly refined skill can only be accomplished from a state of God Awareness or what we call the God State. When one has developed their higher consciousness through contemplation and spiritual exercises and crosses that invisible barrier between the lower and higher worlds, then they enter that state at which the limitations of the gross physical world fall away and all is in a condition of readiness and creative receptivity. In the God State, one encounters a fluid reality that instantly responds to your thoughts and desires, thus manifesting whatever is in your consciousness. There is no time delay as in the physical world because you are operating from a place above space and time. What you create in the God State will eventually manifest in the Lower Worlds, because all physical reality has its source or "counterpart" in the spiritual worlds. Thus what you create while in the state of God Awareness will also create the facsimile of itself on the Physical Plane. The God State allows you to create from the highest elements of divine love and joy which opens up limitless possibilities of manifestation. The Masters of this art can create gardens of living produce on earth that can feed the hungry masses, simply by changing the alchemy of the inner structure of physical reality with the use of their focused will. However, this is only an example of the higher form of Manifestation that can be utilized when one is in the God State and is not generally put to use because of the physical laws that must be adhered to in the Lower Worlds. The Lords of Karma would not look kindly on the use of this art to change the karmic lessons and Life Contracts of the people of Earth, but it illustrates a small portion of the potential of the Art of Manifestation in the true State of God Awareness. For now, use your creativity to make the world around you a little better in whatever capacity brings you joy and pleasure; cultivate the arts of loving expression on Earth and in your heart, and you will be among those who will one day reach the highest forms of art and manifestation in the spiritual worlds of beauty and love where all is in a continual state of divine, receptive creativity.

Herein follows a contemplative exercise with a mantra for energetically collapsing the effects of reoccurring q and karmic loops

1. Imagine you are sitting within a pool of swirling, silver and pink light. It feels like a warm, caressing liquid, but is actually made up of dancing particles of light that sparkle with life and intelligence.

2. Imagine the challenges and karmic loops within your consciousness as ropes around your physical body and allow the swirling waters to loosen and dissolve those ropes, one by one. See them actually break and drop from your body and disappear forever into the shining, silvery pink, living vortex of energy that surrounds and supports you.

3. As you watch the ropes disappear, say this mantra: "**VO-LE-TU-SA-MANA-TE**" (pronounced "voh lay too sah mahnah tay") three times.

4. Do this exercise every day for five days. Thereafter, do it whenever you feel the need for reinforcement or simply for relaxation and rejuvenation. Blessed be to all followers of the Light and Sound of God.

~ ♥ ~

~ Chapter Four ~

Prophecy, the Art of Seeing Beyond the Veil

~ ♥ ~

Nothing is more adventurous than knowing and developing the course of future events on this planet, and be assured that nothing is more carefully monitored than the use of this skill.

~ ♥ ~

The meaning and the divine use of prophecy

Most people think of prophecy as gazing into crystal balls and reading fortunes from Tarot cards. That is a form of "inner seeing" that is limited to the psychic regions of the Astral Plane. It is a highly unreliable method of divination because of the instability of the information coming through. To see with true clarity, one must go beyond the lower planes of transitory reality into the pure, spiritual realms of the Soul Plane and above. This is where the true art of Prophecy has its origin.

Prophecy reaches into the innermost truth behind all things and is the hidden Eye of God that can only be revealed by a master of the Ninth Circle and above. An initiate of the Soul Plane can begin to learn this highly refined skill, but will not be able to fully wield the sword of its power until he or she has studied for many years under a Master of Prophecy and until he or she has become a **tenured resident of the Ninth Plane** of existence. This plane in the God Worlds renders the God seeker immense wisdom and knowledge of the universe. With the Ninth initiation comes the proper level of vibration needed to control the use of this ancient and powerful skill.

The true meaning of Prophecy is the ability to look at the cause of an event before it occurs, not the event itself, but the **cause.** This is the difference between ordinary psychic ability and prophetic vision, because the latter goes beyond the superficial occurrences of life and into their real meaning. When you understand the meaning of the thing that is coming, you can clearly discern it from among the many probable futures constantly forming in the ethers and waiting for a chance to manifest. Not all of "what may be" is going to see the light of day on Earth and so it takes a supercharged and skilled focus of attention to be able to discern which reality is the one that will actually occur. You must understand the nature of that reality and its purpose before it can be revealed to your Inner awareness. This skill takes years of training because of the fickleness of time and events in the Lower Worlds. Those persons with ordinary clairvoyance can only scratch the surface of possible happenings. For instance, they can see a marital partner coming your way in six months, but during that time frame a lot can happen because of the contingencies of free will on both of your parts. It is possible to say to someone, "You will get married," but it is not possible to say exactly when or to whom. However, one who is skilled in the Art of Prophecy can look at the Soul Records and Life Contracts of the two individuals and very accurately predict their life destinies. And here we are getting into the most important aspect of Prophecy – seeing beyond the veil of Maya and into the truth of all life and existence in the Lower Worlds.

True prophetic vision takes place in the God Worlds where history is already completed and waiting to play out in the Theatre of Life. When you can tap into the vast reservoir of knowledge of the finished creations of God, all of life reveals itself as a play or movie that you can forward to the next minute, next scene, or all the way to the end to see in advance what will happen. As you can see, one cannot play with prophetic vision like a child plays with an Ouija board; this talent has the ability to change the destinies of individuals, groups, nations, and planets. It is so far-reaching in its scope that only a very few Masters have been given the sacred knowledge of God's Sight for use and control of karmic evolution and destiny in the Lower Worlds. That is its true purpose; Prophesy is to be used as a guiding and adjusting tool to keep Best-Laid Plans in alignment with the vision and goals of the Supreme God who has created this universe with love and joyful anticipation of reunion with Its beloved ones who are making their way back to It in the choices they make moment by moment each day. Those with the gift of Prophecy are entrusted with the sacred task of helping to guide the course of humanity and to keep it on track as this magnificent theatre of the Lower Worlds closes its curtains one last time and all is restored to a state of perfection and bliss that is its destiny.

Prophecy has been the source of central focus throughout the history of humanity

Mankind has always been moved by an unconscious intuition of knowing what to do and what not to do in any given situation. All forward movement depends upon making the right choices at the right time, and the correct decisions can mean the difference between fortune and misfortune, conquest and defeat, or freedom and slavery. Great nations have risen and fallen according to the decisions made by their leaders. It has been that way since ancient times and is still very relevant today, even with the development of "remote viewing" by investigative agencies. Thus, human beings have been consulting with oracles and seers since the beginning of the history of this planet.

Paramitas, the Gathering of Many Rivers

Knowledge is power, and foresight gives that power additional and tremendous force to change and control events. Over the centuries, the most basic drive in human nature has been to create wealth and prosperity; to wield victory over our enemies, and to claim as much territory and precious resources of this Earth as possible. Prophecy is the coveted Ace in the deck of cards that mankind has long pursued in its quest to win dominion over the Earth. Kings of old had their own seers as part of their household, and these people who professed to know the future were given great authority and latitude to influence the course of events between kingdoms and nations.

There have been many times in history where leaders of men would not make a political or strategic military move without first consulting the advice of an oracle. There is unlimited power in knowing the future, so the mysterious and precious Art of Prophetic Vision has long been a central point of focus in the historical evolution of the Lower Worlds. Much of its original splendor has been lost however, in the current age of machinery and technology, especially with the onset of "computer wisdom" via the Internet, which is the new oracle of the modern age, but the heart of true prophecy still pulses within the primal consciousness of man and he will always be drawn toward lifting the veil that separates the conditions of the present from the promise of the future.

The difference between Prophetic Vision, which emanates from the lower Temporal Worlds and that which comes from the God Worlds

This difference is all a matter of the quality and strength of the degree of vibration; the higher the vibration, the stronger, more accurate and more expansive is the level of prophecy. In the lower vibratory substance of the temporal worlds, all is in a continual state of flux due to the laws of cause and effect and the contingencies of free will. It is therefore difficult to make accurate predictions unless they occur within minutes of an event and the closer one gets to an event, the harder it is to "pinpoint" it in time and space. Seen from a distance of weeks or months, it is like a large panoramic scene of moving images that one with Prophetic Vision can watch playing out on the movie screen of probable futures from the etheric realms of thought and manifestation, but the closer this scene gets to manifesting in physical reality, the smaller it becomes, until it is merely a speck of light floating down from space. Only one who is fully trained in this Art is able to distinguish this approaching occurrence from the ever changing, moving images of events that surround it. The most accurate predictions are those that can be made minutes or hours before the event, and very few souls are skilled in this aspect of prophecy. Most people who espouse to know the future make predictions that are months or years in advance and in the Lower Worlds this leads to a high degree of inaccuracy and failure, as "reality" is always in a condition of fluctuation and instability.

Prophetic Vision which emanates from the God Worlds captures the expansiveness of that realm in which there is no time and space; all is happening at once in the everlasting Now. What appears as a panorama in the Lower Worlds becomes something infinitely larger and without boundaries when seen from the God State. Prophetic Vision from this perspective takes in ALL of what has been and what is yet to be manifested in the worlds above and below the Great Divide. It is like seeing from 360 degrees in all directions at once and knowing all past, present and future states of reality. From this vantage point it is easy to locate a specific occurrence and how and when it will manifest in the temporal worlds; so one who is to be trained in this divine art of Inner seeing must first be very accomplished in USM and familiar with the spiritual laws that govern this universe. They must be of mastership status to enter this training that is similar to that of the Silent Nine, in which complete secrecy, silence, and trust must be maintained at all times for the magnitude of the vision of God's Own Heart to be revealed to the eyes of that soul. What is the purpose for which this kind of prophetic vision is bestowed and utilized? It is to help regulate and propagate the unfoldment of the universal life plans for this Sugmad and this universe by the One Father of All, who sees without seeing and knows without knowing, and from whom all universal truths and visions flow and have their being.

The Lords of Karma utilize Prophetic Vision to shape historical events

The Lords of Karma have long used the tool of prophecy to control and shape the course of historical events on Earth. This is done in accordance with the will and plans of the One Father God. The progress of humanity is regularly and closely monitored by the Masters of the Inner realms who work closely with the Lords of Karma to insure that all human activity stays within given guidelines that are highly flexible, yet have certain boundaries that cannot be crossed. If an event is of the kind that would exceed the limitations as set by the Lords of Karma, it must be adjusted so as not to cross into the "danger zone" which is an area of the universe that has no spiritual jurisdiction and is like the swamp lands that swallow souls into their murky depths. This "no man's land" was created to give balance to the high grounds of the spiritual worlds and is literally a dumping ground for those souls who would interfere with the overall safety and advancement of the human race.

It is a rare occurrence that a soul of truly evil intent will exist and find itself banished in this way. Adolf Hitler was one such soul whose evil plot to destroy human life was seen far in advance by the use of Prophetic Vision in the chambers of the Lords of Karma. They allowed him to perpetrate the atrocities of the Holocaust in order to balance the group karma of the Jewish peoples. However, he was only allowed to go only so far before they stepped in and dismantled his plans for world destruction. Though humanity's divine gift of free will has given license to enslavement, destruction, genocide and war, there is no human action outside the scope of God's All-Knowingness. God knows what choices soul will make before they are enacted, **It will, nevertheless, respect our use of divine free will until our free will disturbs the universal balance of creation.**

Had the Lords of Karma not used the Art of Prophecy, Hitler's blight would have eventually covered the entire Earth, so great was his alliance with the Forces of Darkness. Be not fooled; Hitler was only a puppet of the True Power that used him, and his life was a tragic example of a lost soul crossing the bounds of human decency and falling into the danger zone of the Outer Worlds.

There have been many instances of the misuse of power being significantly altered, diminished, or thwarted entirely from the application of Prophetic Vision by those who govern the sanctity of God's plans for the progress of humanity. Evil is only allowed to exist in order for karmic debt and destiny to play out so that the goals of balancing this universe will always be met.

The Lords of Karma conferred Nostradamus with the gift of "Seeing Beyond the Veil"

Nostradamus was chosen because of his unique understanding of the movements of planetary and solar systems. This ability widened his knowledge of the magnetic field of energy that forms a circumference around the universe and is what attracts and repels events that wait to enter the Earth's atmosphere. He could mathematically determine the probability and timing of an event by its position in relation to the energy fields of the stars and planets. To Nostradamus' Inner vision, an event awaiting manifestation was as "solid" as any one of the heavenly bodies that appeared in his telescope, and existed in the same relative space and time. He could see the event with the same clarity that he could watch a comet diving across the sky to Earth. Many of his prophetic visions existed in the far future, and some were too powerful to be openly revealed. Thus, he wrote about them in verse that was deliberately oblique and open to multiple interpretations. Even today, only a fraction of the true body of Nostradamus' prophecies has ever been made public. The rest were constructed in number codes to protect their powerful vibratory structure and ability to change the course of history from the eyes of the profane that would abuse that knowledge and cause great damage to the fabric of universal integrity and balance. The world of his day was not ready for the explosive potency of this group of prophecies coming through his Inner vision. These prophesies are stored in codes of numbers that will one day be deciphered when the time has come for the light of their revelation.

The training of prophecy in Ekere Tere

This training is accessible only to initiates of the Ninth Circle and above, for only those with the proper level of knowledge and vibration can be trusted with holding the future of the world in their hands. The Art of Prophecy has the power to change the destinies of individuals and nations, planets and solar systems. One must be meticulously trained in its use in order to fully understand its multi-dimensional fabric and scope. The nature of this training is secret and is done on the Inner planes of the God Worlds. There is a Master named Lu Ten who works with souls who are ready to enter their apprenticeship in learning the Art of Prophecy, and he can be located in the spiritual city of Ekere Tere, that has been established by the Living Master to make these ancient, esoteric teachings more accessible to those who are ready to embark on adventures on a grand scale. Nothing is more adventurous than knowing and developing the course of future events on this planet, and be assured that nothing is more carefully monitored than the use of this skill. Very few souls who begin the study of true prophecy ever finish the regiment of tests; they often veer off into flights of ego and dreams of power. No one is immune to the siren call of Maya when it sings so sweetly in the human consciousness, and it takes great spiritual strength of character to stay on track and in alignment with the higher good of Divine Plans. Training is also quite rigorous. It is similar to "boot camp," as the endurance of soul is tested in many different ways; "testing your mettle" applies very accurately here. Training in the Art of Prophesy is on par with the Living Master's training because it entails being given the trust of the heart of God in the future and survival of this universe.

Universal Soul Movement is the first step toward opening the Third Eye to the finer vibrations of the unseen realms and to "seeing beyond the veil." Universal Soul Movement conditions the heart to hold more love, and provides the protection and preparation necessary to become familiar with the beings and laws and territories souls will encounter in their Inner travels and observations as they pursue mastering the Art of Prophecy. It helps to know the grounds you are walking on and what to expect at each turn when venturing into unknown regions that hold the secrets to universal truths and the origin of prophetic visions.

Degrees of prophecy

There are three degrees of prophecy:

1) The ability to change the present by going back in time to change the present without disturbing karmic balances.

2) The ability to change the present through prophetic sight of events about to happen within moments of their occurrence.

3) The ability to utilize the Prophetic vision of major planetary changes and significant historical personalities which will be coming into the world.

The **first degree of prophecy** is the most sought after because *everyone wants "a second chance" to do things over and make them right.* In hindsight people can see their mistakes and sometimes it is only one small thing that would have made the difference in the entire scope of their lives thereafter. So, they wish to go back and do it again with what they know now. "If only I had done it that way," and "I wonder what would have happened if I had not done that," are the most common of human ponderings and yearnings. This is natural and part of the growing process as souls make their way through the labyrinth of their worldly experiences. And so the question is "Can we go back in time and change the past to create a better future without disturbing karmic balances?" Yes and no. We can always go back in time once we understand how to manipulate the time track through USM. Time is merely a commodity for use in the Lower Worlds to organize daily activities and make sense of life's forward movement. Time does not exist in the worlds of God and Spirit, and so it can be lifted from the Third Eye like a curtain is lifted from a window, and one can see the larger view into the screen of the eternal now, where past, present and future meet together in one ever-moving reality. You can view all the events of your life, from past lives and all the way up until this time, as images on a movie screen. You can call on Master Shamus Tabriz to assist you in gathering these scenes from your lifetimes from his records in the Akashic Library on the Causal Plane. All you have ever thought, felt and done has been recorded in this library of the Inner Worlds and can be called back for review and change. Yes, you can review a past incident and **change** its vibrations in order to structurally alter the effects of your present circumstances. Shamus can show you how to do this. So, changing an event of the past is rather an easy thing to do if you have a good grasp of USM.

However, there is another aspect of this to consider. Any changes made to past events that have already been resolved and written into the annals of the Akashic records and personal or human history will carry the karmic responsibility of the one seeking them and must therefore have the approval of the Lords of Karma. If the change falls into alignment with the higher good of all who would be affected by it and would not cause a breach in the Best-

Laid Plans for this planet and universe, then it could be approved and played out. We are all making choices every moment of the day and there are many different choices that have various outcomes in the activity of free will, so there is nothing set in stone as to the "right" or "only" choice or destiny for any human being. It is acceptable to go back and make a different choice, so long as it falls within the margins of the Life Contracts of all concerned, and does not radically go outside of your agreement with Spirit to pursue your highest goals in this incarnation. For instance, the choosing of another life partner would send you down a completely different path with different souls interacting in your life, and other circumstances to be met. This is perfectly acceptable if it allows for the unfolding of life agreements for all concerned and does not interfere with the overall karmic fabric of the lives of those souls. There are many ways to resolve karma and the Lords of Karma can be quite flexible and creative in working with souls to achieve their greatest potential and fulfillment in life. These Holy Ones have deep compassion for the human consciousness and are always willing to work with sincere souls who strive to find their highest truth while traveling the paths of past, present and future as they make their way back to the Sea of deep Mercy and Love in the eternal Now.

The **second degree of prophecy** entails the ability to see an event coming within moments of its occurrence. This is a very highly skilled talent because, as we have discussed earlier, the closer an event comes into being, the harder it is to distinguish it from other events that float in the ethers awaiting manifestation. One must have the ability to "zero in" on the magnetic resonance of this particular occurrence and make a lightning-fast decision about its nature and effect. Each event waiting to happen actually sends out a signal that makes a very particular sound that grows louder as the timing moves closer to its arrival. One who is skilled in the art of prophecy can discern this signal and quickly interpret its meaning. The signal also carries a "picture" of what is coming so that it can be evaluated and preparations can be made to alter or intercept the conditions surrounding its materialization as necessary, but we can take this one step further. There are those Masters in the prophetic arts who can *alter an event at the beginning of its formation* by tuning in on the earliest signal of its development and completely *silencing the signal,* thus eradicating the event and preventing it from ever growing into maturity, or "nipping it in the bud."

A natural question about the above would be, "If this kind of ability exists, why do so many bad things happen in the world?" Again, it is a matter of keeping balance in a world of cause and effect, and of noninterference with the karmic destiny and Life Contracts of its inhabitants. However, there is room for great flexibility in the way that dramas can play out on the world stage, which is why many events have been altered and many have never even seen the light of day. Be assured that as "bad" as things may sometimes seem, they could have been much worse, as the Kal forces continually plot to carry out acts of violence and destruction on the earth, but the hand of God has often intervened to thwart darkness with the grace of the supreme gift of Prophetic Sight to those few trusted souls who can use it wisely, and with compassion and love for humanity and its sacred goal to return safely to the arms of the Divine.

The **third degree of prophecy** is (a) the ability to foresee major planetary changes and (b) the ability to know the arrival of those souls who would have significant impact on the history of the world. The first part of these insights indicates a uniquely interesting talent and requires something quite different from the other degrees of prophetic vision. The soul who employs this first skill is often in league with extra-terrestrial beings that exist in other universes and are the guardians at the gates of interplanetary unity and harmony. The soul who interacts with these beings must be highly skilled in USM and familiar with other forms of life that may appear radically different from those of Earth, and even appear as frightening or threatening. These beings have been given this kind of outer garment to fulfill their duties as guardians who ward off or "scare away" beings of self-serving or malicious intent, or those who are simply curious to see beyond the gates. The one skilled in prophetic arts works in harmony with these other-worldly beings to monitor the progress and changes of the course of the planets in each cosmic system. Such souls are not limited to one universe, but can also take part in the balance of planetary harmony in other universes as well. They often work closely with the Living Master of the times whose duty it is to continue the progress of universal balance and alignment with the will of this Sugmad (or God), and of other Sugmads who oversee other universes. So you can see that this is a very far reaching, expansive skill with many interactive parts and players. Only one of mastership status can use this skill effectively for the good of planetary monitoring and adjustments. One advantage of this prophetic talent is the ability to prevent a "crashing of planets" whose orbits may have been thrown off during one of the many magnetic storms that occur regularly in the cosmos. This soul not only has the ability to see the catastrophe ahead of time, but also can work closely with those others who can alter the course of planetary movements and changes to maintain the balance of each universal life cycle and its structural integrity.

The second part of the third degree of prophecy entails the foreseeing of historical figures coming into the world. This is a skill that requires cooperation and agreement with the Lords of Karma for permission to view a soul's Life Contract and Akashic records. One may catch a "glimpse" of the potential of a soul who is incarnating into the world, but to truly "know" its destiny requires viewing these records with a Master like Shamus Tabriz and it is only for the benefit of the progress of humanity that the incoming soul's destiny would be revealed. Even so, there is no guarantee that the individual will fulfill their given role in the world because of the nature of contingencies and free will that are always at play, but more likely than not, one who is destined for historical greatness will strive to fulfill that role because they are encouraged and guided by those masters who are assigned to watch over their progress. And the one who is skilled at the art of prophecy works alongside these guardians to "make the way clear" for the incoming historical figures by helping to align events in the most optimal way for the successful completion of the karmic destiny of those individuals in history.

Few God seekers master all three degrees of prophecy

It is a masterful undertaking to tackle skills of this magnitude and most people shrink from the responsibility and karmic implications of dabbling with the past, present and future of individual lives and of the world at large. Even the planetary and solar systems can be affected by prophetic wisdom and the decisions made therefrom. And so it is with very careful planning that the Lords of Karma work with the goals of our Sugmad to pick and choose the right candidates to bear the mantle of prophetic vision and knowledge. Once chosen, the candidates must be interviewed by those Masters who are in charge of overseeing the progress and balance of universal concerns, including the Living Master, the Nine Silent Ones, and members of the Grand Council, including Milarepa and Master Paul Twitchell. It is similar to a job applicant who is applying for a major position with a multi-million dollar corporation. The interviews are intense and meant to weed out the "maybe's" from the "will do's." We can discern a lot during these exchanges with our candidates, and they are allowed to ask as many questions as needed, so that it becomes a dialogue and not an interrogation. All is done within the context of love and support, but it is tough love that is rendered and applied. Once a candidate has been chosen, they are given an apprenticeship with one of the Masters of the prophetic arts, and their training then begins. The length of the training period depends upon the individual, but generally can take from ten to twenty years. Part of this training involves the study of how time and space operate along with the Laws of Karma in the Lower Worlds, so that the proper choices and decisions can be made with any given situation in which the Art of Prophecy will be applied. It takes many experiments working with these and other related elements within a classroom environment to test the understanding and wisdom of the apprentice as he or she makes his or her way to the platform of the genuine purposes and uses of Prophecy. Then and only then will they be allowed to test their wings in flight toward true mastership of prophetic vision as it applies to the love, compassion, protection and guidance of humanity and the balance of universal harmony and fulfillment of Best-Laid Plans.

Members of the White, Grey, and Lavender Robes are also trained in the Art of Prophecy

Candidates are chosen by a panel of Masters who work with the Silent Nine in the Wisdom Temple of Le He in the city of Prahana Let on the Etheric Plane. Each candidate is carefully screened to determine his or her spiritual merits and worthiness to carry this mantle. They must pass many rigorous tests of fortitude, endurance and willingness to serve Sugmad to the utmost of their abilities. Candidates are chosen because of their proven obedience to the laws that govern the universe and their ability to withstand the storms of the human mind and ego and maintain Inner peace and balance at all times.

Training for the prophetic arts has been in existence for millennia of your time and long before recorded history. There is actually no time reference that can be given, so ancient is this art and its instruction. The length of training depends upon the spiritual background of each candidate and can be from six to twenty years in duration. The instruction is overseen by members of the White Robes who are working with the Silent Nine to sustain the maintenance of this universe and its proper function. The successful completion of the training period is determined by a vote of the Grand Council that weighs the merits of each student in accordance with the advisement of their instructors. The spiritual skills that are reviewed and must be mastered to attain graduation are truthfulness, integrity, forthrightness, valor, perseverance, accountability and proper discernment.

This training of select members preserves the balance of Sugmad's contract with the Father of All by releasing the protective forces of prophetic wisdom and vision into the universe to aid in sustaining Earth's evolution toward the completion of its life cycle. Sugmad wants to "bring it home" – this magnificent creation of life, beauty, love, joy and truth, of which the grand Art of Prophecy is a major part of the matriculation and graduation of Its Dream and Heart and is a Supreme Gift to Its Father.

The question of end times

The chaos and other calamities that have already befallen the Earth are in actuality a preview of the true destruction that is potential and yet to come. They are like a foreshadowing of events yet in the making. *We can stop the trajectory of these events with the use of prophetic vision, as that has always been its purpose*: to keep the universe in balance so that evil cannot topple everything

Sugmad has been building for eons. What we have considered to be enormous destruction in this world is nothing compared to what the dark forces would like to carry out, which is the complete annihilation of the Earth and its inhabitants. The reason this has not already happened is because the Masters who govern this universe use the Art of Prophecy to stay ahead of the plans of darkness and thwart them enough to keep the balance of life ever moving forward and in alignment with the divine vision and destiny as laid out by our God, the Sugmad, as It seeks to bring this dream of creation to its glorious conclusion. Nothing can truly stand in the way of the goals of the One Great God before whom even the forces of darkness must kneel. This is all one enormous drama being played out in the theatre of life and the Director calls the final shots and determines how they will be delivered. Any time It wants to, our God can close the curtains on this grand universal play of creation, but It has given Its actors free will to interpret their parts and has given them the tools to make the play either a great success, or drive it to failure. The use of prophetic vision is the final act in the drama on this world stage that will determine its ultimate fate.

Armageddon and Judgment Day

"The End Is Near" has been posted on signs and cried out in warnings for many centuries of man's existence. Doomsday warnings are like a call to arms for the human conscience to redeem itself before it is too late. Persons who have spouted these dire predictions have been met with ridicule and derision, but they are merely reflecting the growing unrest within the collective consciousness of the world and its inhabitants: a feeling of guilt over past actions or of those not taken, and the fear of having to pay the price of spiritual punishment when the life is reviewed as the soul stands trembling before the fires of retribution on judgment day.

The knowledge that there will one day be the "last day" in a human being's life and that it is ever looming in the prophecies that describe the end times of the world does influence the manner in which humans conduct themselves on a daily basis. They are ever wondering how their current choices of actions will affect them down the road. "Act now and pay later" is a common thought in the average mentality, along with an awareness that actions reap consequences that must be addressed at some future time. This understanding is what has prevented utter chaos from erupting all across the face of the Earth, the intuitive knowledge that you cannot really get away with anything because everyone will have their day of reckoning. This is a fear-based theology that is an upside down version of the Law of Karma which states that for every action there must be an equal and opposite reaction to restore balance to the universe. Fearful or not, this theological perception of fire and brimstone is the rudimentary stepping stone to the growth of the collective human consciousness. All must move forward from darkness to light, and divine guidance will use whatever it takes to get all souls to the next place of spiritual progress. This understanding of end times and paying the piper is one of the most powerful forces influencing human actions around the world. It is helping to keep the journey of soul in alignment with the will of The Father as humanity struggles each day to steady and redeem its course through choices that will insure its survival as a species on Earth and as returning spiritual beings finding their true place in the heavenly worlds. The end-times is a transition in mankind's genetic make-up due to changes in the chemical composition of the Earth and its ecosystem.

Here follows a spiritual exercise that will develop the soul's ability to intuit the truth in personal matters and events

1. Imagine you are sitting before a full-length mirror with a clear view of yourself. See that a light is shining over your head; it is golden with deep orange tones.

2. Allow yourself to float into this light and become one with its warm, pulsing energy. This is the light of your own awareness and ability to discern the truth behind all the events in your life.

3. Keep watching your image bathed in this light as you sit in front of your Inner mirror and chant this mantra three times: **"RAY-SO-LA-TE-MAY-TO"** (pronounced "ray so lah tay may toe.")

4. Now call forth one of the Masters of the Sehaji with whom you feel a close rapport and ask him or her to show you an image of the truth behind any person, event, or situation in your life that you wish to understand. Ask your question and then keep your Inner eyes focused on your mirror and watch as it clouds over with mist. After a few minutes the mist begins to clear and you will see an image slowly come into focus. It

may be a literal answer to your question, or it may be something symbolic for you to interpret with your Master Teacher. You may also get a word or sentence or even a story about your question. This may come now or at a later time when you are busy with your daily activities or when you are resting. When it comes, write it down in your journal. If you do not understand the answer to your question, take it into contemplation and ask for clarification. Your truth will be made known to you. Blessed be.

~ ♥ ~

Paramitas, the Gathering of Many Rivers

~ Chapter Five ~

Exploring Uncharted Lands

~ ♥ ~

A glimpse of the true worlds of God will make your earthly gains seem insignificant and unsatisfying. You will crave more of heaven with every movement towards its magnificent, shining gates.

~ ♥ ~

The ultimate goal of Universal Soul Movement

The ultimate goal of Universal Soul Movement (USM) is to reconnect soul with its lost heritage, that of being an heir to the Kingdom of Heaven. The purpose of USM is to ignite the memory of soul's origin as it flew out of the body of its Father, becoming a separate entity and yet One with the heart of Imagination and Creativity. Love is the force behind all that was created and soul is the bearer of that love in the universes of God. Soul must remember its true nature, and all is revealed in time through the art of USM. This is a highly profound and yet simple movement of consciousness from the realm of the ordinary physical reality to the higher and finer aspects of divine consciousness. For instance, one can use it while driving the car and watching the road transform into an open highway to the God Worlds by simply chanting HU or any other word of spiritual power and substance with the ability to connect one's awareness to the heartbeat of God. That is all that is required for basic USM - to chant, to open the heart, refine the focus, clear the road, and envision Heaven. Some people make a practice of inwardly chanting the holy words all day long. It is not necessary to give up your daily life and responsibilities and retreat to a mountain top in the Himalayas. It is not required to throw away your belongings and don the robes of poverty and renunciation. That is not the way of the God of Abundance and Love. You may keep your houses, cars, garments and jewels, and you may enjoy the harvest of worldly prosperity and pleasures. This garden was created for your delight and enjoyment; the fruits fall from the trees at your feet and it is your divine right to partake of them.

Universal Soul Movement requires only that you practice it daily in the form that is right for you so that you can grow into your higher consciousness and see heaven in your lifetime. A glimpse of the true worlds of God will make your earthly gains seem insignificant and unsatisfying. You will crave more of heaven with every movement towards its magnificent, shining gates.

The proper use of USM will ultimately lead the seeker to the place we call the Uncharted Lands. Achieving this is simply a matter of applying focused discipline and perseverance in using the spiritual techniques and exercises as given by the Living Master, and of **never giving up.** It is too easy to grow frustrated and say, "This doesn't work." It is the soul who keeps trying, who forges ahead past all obstacles and practices daily the precious gems of spiritual wisdom provided in books like this who will begin to see past the veils upon veils of Maya (illusion) clouding their vision and be rewarded with a view of Eternal Mystery and Majesty. These lands are not for the faint of heart, my friend. Their revelations will only be won by those souls who have proven their fearless commitment to finding truth and freedom. The journey begins with a shift in consciousness in one's own heart. Do you know how vast is the mystery and beauty of the worlds within you as soul? Do you know that it takes not one physical step from where you are to have a world open up before you that you could not envision in your wildest fantasy? Universal Soul Movement teaches individuals to find the Uncharted Lands within their own Beingness because that is where it all begins and ends, Dear One. If you look deeply, deeply within your Self, then that is the doorway you seek toward reunion with Divine Love, Mercy and Joy. It is not in a desert or mountain or ocean; it is in your own heart. God gave you the key; you have always owned it. Use it. Unlock the worlds within you; they await your presence.

Universal Soul Movement (USM) relates closely to prayer, meditation and the use of mantras

Prayer, meditation and chanting words of spiritual merit or mantras are the stepping stones to USM. As very small children, many of you were taught how to pray with hands clasped together and eyes closed; blessing your mother and father, brothers and sisters, and asking God for His love and protection. This was your first step toward moving outside the boundaries of your physical world and putting your trust in something much larger than yourself. You were developing faith in the invisible presence of God. It is this faith that is the sustaining force behind all forms of prayer and petitions to the Holy Spirit and it is what gives mantras their positive energy. And it is this faith that underlies the guiding power of USM, which is actually a higher form of prayer and meditation. With USM one casts all doubt to the winds and takes the leap from the cliff with the full expectation of soaring over the canyons below. In this mode of consciousness, one is not only praying to God, but is interacting with the very heart of Creation. The difference between traditional prayer and the active use of contemplation through USM is that with prayer you say, "God, come to me," and in USM you say, "I am coming to God."

Universal Soul Movement is an active form of prayer in which imagination and creativity play key roles. You can use a spiritual exercise as given by a master such as the Living Master, or you can create your own exercise with the use of your imagination. Whether you take a "guided tour" or venture on your own into the spiritual realms, the key to any successful forward movement of consciousness is to **have faith and trust in your own experiences.** This begins with a mantra, such as HU, which is an ancient name for God that has a very high and pure vibration. The use of this word when spoken with an open heart filled with love is the launching pad for USM and soul will literally take off and fly into the upper spiritual planes far above and beyond the gross reality of the physical world. You may find yourself visiting a temple of wisdom, or communing with a Master, or catching images of past lives or of future lives yet to come. This is where faith becomes the crucial factor within your travels because nobody can validate your experiences; they are yours and yours alone. When you learn to trust what comes to you and build that into your daily existence, you are growing in spiritual strength and confidence in your ability to gain wisdom, love and understanding from the divine source within your own consciousness. Spiritual power is not about controlling anything or anyone outside of yourself; it is about the awareness of your oneness with All That Is. It is to BE, KNOW and SEE who you are as a child of God, and to have Faith and Trust in the eternal, unbreakable bond of that divine relationship as you move through the maze of time and space in the lower planes of existence toward your true home in the highest heavenly worlds of pure Spirit, Love and Truth.

How humanity was led in its very beginnings by Spirit to develop prayer, meditation, and contemplation as a means to petition and dialogue with God

When man first learned how to create fire, he began to worship the blaze of his creation because he intuitively recognized the "divine spark" within each flame that dazzled his eyes, warmed his body, and cooked his food. Fire was the first god that was formally worshipped by humanity and then other gods of the earth, water and sky were given great power and reverence in the mind and heart of man. It was the **belief** in these gods and goddesses that gave them the power to heal and protect those who revered them. Man created many of the gods he worshipped from within his own consciousness and they took on the life and personalities with which they were bestowed by the human mind. This is not meant to say that all gods were figments of projected thought; but the majority of those that were given homage by our primitive forefathers lived and breathed by the imagination and belief in their existence.

As early man called forth the images of his gods, he created a system of prayerful invocations and incantations that were the first forms of prayer, chants, and meditation. In many cases, contemplation was used, but not consciously. Men and women caught in the throes of powerful emotions as their bodies swayed to the chanting rhythms of voices, drums and other instruments of invocation, were often taken "out of the body" as in astral projection. And it was often the case that the travel of soul was confined to the astral world. However, many spiritual chiefs and shamans, and those who were highly intuitive or sensitive would move into the realm of contemplation and experience USM, which took them well beyond the lower planes of reality. It was rather a **spontaneous experience** and not governed by the structure of a religious doctrine. In fact, the major religions of this world are what have kept man in a continual state of spiritual ignorance and stagnancy by their restrictive and judgmental orthodoxy based on the fear and not the love of God.

Man in his natural state has always had the ability to move beyond the physical consciousness and to see into the true worlds of spirit. He was given a homing device by the One True Father that is part of his basic genetic code, or DNA. This is like a "golden cord" that connects soul to its Father and divine origins at all times. That cord has been seriously compromised by the religious rhetoric forced upon humanity by the Church and its leaders who have largely used religion not to help man reunite with his spiritual heritage and freedom, but to keep him controlled and enslaved by the power of greed that has seeped into the foundation of the major religions of this earth. The attempt to keep humanity in darkness has given great power to the spiritual leaders of these faiths who have demanded more and more money and obedience to keep their religious dynasties strong and powerful. The Church has long held an iron grip upon the consciousness of humanity; it is time now to relax that vise and for mankind to resume its own unique and sacred relationship with God and heaven.

From earliest times, Spirit has worked with the heart of each person on earth to keep their golden cord to God strong and vibrating with the Light and Sound that will naturally guide and pull them back to the arms of Love and Mercy. It is this light that overcomes all dark forces and in the end all will be returned to the natural state of Grace and Perfection that is the dream of the Heavenly Father above.

The Uncharted Lands in the Worlds Unseen

The Uncharted Lands are the Inner landscapes of the spiritual consciousness that can only be accessed through direct contact with a spiritual master of very high merit who can be your guide through the worlds upon worlds of majesty and mystery that await your exploration. One can explore these territories alone, but then there is the risk of falling into "danger zones" and mixing with unsavory beings who may wish to do you harm. It is best to have a guide who is familiar with these unseen worlds that exist just beyond the rim of your conscious awareness.

Some of what you may see in the Uncharted Lands of the Inner realms are planets not known to your solar system that do not adhere to the same physical laws of time, space and gravity. They are inhabited by beings that may look like some of the creatures depicted in mythology and science fiction fantasy; they do not have human features and some of them do not have a conscience as we know it of "right and wrong" but conduct themselves purely by instinct and the drive for survival and conquest. Some of these planets or worlds are of a warring nature and would like to intrude upon the Earth's solar system, which is heavily guarded by a legion of soldiers under the command of Master Tindor Saki. He has done an excellent job of protecting the Earth's atmosphere from hostile invasion and maintained the sanctity of life in the physical realms.

Other planets in the Uncharted Lands are of a more harmonious nature and inhabited by beings that love the Earth and humanity and have often come here in various guises to assist mankind in its daily and worldly challenges. These beings have often been mistaken for "angels" because of their benevolent appearance and manner. Some of them appear as nature fairies that populate the forests of countries like Germany, France, England and Spain. Their intention is to bring balance to the Earth through union with all life that is "rooted" to the soil and thereby spread love and strength to the very core of this planet. The Earth is a being that has a soul and evolution of its own, and it is very important for the progression of humanity to keep Mother Earth in balance and good health. If the very foundation under our feet is compromised or destroyed, we cannot stand and move forward. And so many of these beings from the worlds unseen come here to protect and heal the "charted" lands of the Lower Worlds so that mankind can continue to pursue its journey toward spiritual freedom.

I have been able to describe here only a minute fraction of what these Uncharted Lands entail. Most of it is far beyond what can be conveyed in human language. We like to use the term "lands" but this is somewhat misleading. Yes, there are worlds and planets with living beings as described above, but the vast majority of this Inner landscape is not about other worlds and life forms. The Inner landscape is about the very heart and soul of Creation which reaches into the very fabric of existence itself. It is Light and Sound; it is movement on the currents of life and being. It is about the feeling of oneness with all that is and will be. You have been told about the many planes of existence, the Heavenly Hierarchies and the Guardians and Gods of those worlds. That is all fair and true, but when we move into the true Uncharted Lands of God, we leave all that we know behind us and become as Light itself moving in oneness with the pure Joy of Beingness. That is as close as I can come to describing what it is like to explore this mysterious Inner terrain of consciousness. It is up to each one of you to go beyond your comfort zones and attempt each day in contemplation to expand your ability to perceive and reach for the next step in your understanding. Be ready to take the hand when it is offered to you from the Inner Master who stands by, waiting to show you what lies beyond the curtain of your simple human awareness. Let it part and reveal to you the true Breath of Life and Being; step into the blinding Light and your true vision will be opened with pure and thrilling clarity.

Universal Soul Movement (USM) relates to the activity level of the pineal gland – humanity's Spiritual Eye

The more one's Spiritual Eye opens, the further one can travel in USM. So it is very important to do the spiritual exercises as given by the Living Master, because they stimulate the pineal gland and condition the Spiritual Eye to receive more light, understanding and information from the Inner realms. It is like looking through a kaleidoscope of changing colors and images that are condensed or enhanced by the movement of consciousness of the viewer. And USM opens the living pictures into landscapes and wonders beyond the rim of the viewing scope. The pineal gland works in harmony with USM; they are interdependent, but it does begin with focusing the attention between the eyebrows and using a highly charged spiritual word that will open the Spiritual Eye significantly so that USM can commence.

Mantras are constructed with variances of frequency of the Light and Sound designed specifically for each God seeker

Mantras are constructed with frequencies of the Light and Sound that will resonate uniquely with the individual consciousness of each practitioner. Each mantra is like a key designed to fit the locks within the consciousness of each person, and no two keys are alike. This is the beauty and mystery of how the Light and Sound works one-on-one with each soul in creation. It honors their singular histories and experiences, and calibrates perfectly with their ability to receive the flow of spiritual energy that the mantras will initiate in them. There is a grid of spiritual light within each soul that expands with the vibration of the mantra being used. "One Mantra Fits All" is not too far-fetched as the Light and Sound simply adjusts to the individual state of consciousness as described above. However, it is often more powerful for souls to receive their own special and secret mantras designed especially for them, as by doing so they can find their own true voices in the God Worlds and develop their own unique signatures. This will propel them further and more quickly along the path of their spiritual development. A mantra designed for an individual will more quickly unlock his or her creative soul potential and open them to more Light and Sound as they build their divine house within.

The Master Language in contemplative activity is split into multiples of the trinity, like the numbers 3, 6, 9, 12, 24, 36, 39, 42, and onward to 60

The basic foundation of all life begins with the number three; this is in alignment with the Holy Trinity of the Father, Son and Holy Ghost of the Christian doctrine and the basis of all the major religions on Earth. It is the underlying foundation of all creation; that everything is created in multiples of three, beginning with God, soul, and Spirit. One cannot go into any form of spiritual contemplation or soul movement without the multiples of the Trinity because soul unfolds and moves forward as part of the Trinity with the Father and Holy Spirit; thus it moves in steps of three. This process has a multiplying effect because nothing in the universe remains static; it is always building upon itself. And since the heart of all life begins with the number three, then all that is generated from that point will multiply by that number.

Here follows a contemplative exercise with a mantra that will give the God seeker a glimpse of God Consciousness

1. Imagine sitting in a darkened movie theater. The massive curtains slowly pull away from the screen and there is a bright, white field on which an image will soon come into view.

2. Concentrate on the white screen before you and say this mantra three times: **"SU-LE-TA-VIYU-NAM-SUGMAD"** (pronounced "soo lay tah veeyoo nahm soogmahd.")

3. Simply continue to watch this Inner screen of light until the Face of God begins to appear. It may look like a simple blue spot or circle; or it may look like stars or colored lights; or you may see two brilliant eyes gazing into your heart. Whatever form it takes, The Face of God will always remain a puzzle yet to be completed and does not appear the same way to any two souls, but It will reveal a part of Itself to the true God seeker who is ready for a glimpse of God Consciousness.

Here is a contemplative prayer that will give greater love and understanding of the hearts of others

Father, Make Me More Like You

Father, help me **to see** the light that shines in the heart
Of every soul I encounter throughout my day.
Help me to smile
Into their eyes when there is no kindness or
warmth reflected there,
And let me be the one who offers **the gift
of compassion and mercy.**

This is the time of true Brotherhood on Earth when all souls
Seeking redemption can come together and
find **real understanding**
In our brothers and sisters hearts by
stopping to listen to each other
And **truly hear** what each one has to say.

To **listen with love** is the forgotten art that
brings color and beauty
To the tapestry of life; it is what makes a
palette of grays and blues
Explode into a canvas of brilliant flowers
bathed in sunlight.
Help me listen to my brethren and truly give of
my attention and love.

The **world will open its heart to me** when I
am opened to the world.

Paramitas, the Gathering of Many Rivers

There is **no need for loneliness and despair** if
I will but take the hand
Of the one who is lying in the road and
gently help them to their feet.
Then together we can find the sun that lights
the greater path before us.

Nobody can do it alone in this earthly world; **we
came here together**
To learn to work in **harmony** with each other, and
be each other's cheerleaders
And comfort when the darkness falls so heavy on
our hearts. **Father**, let me find
The true center of love in every heart I encounter by
being a Magnet of **Thy Love.**

Before I go out each day, I will bless the morning and say,
"I give and receive only love."
This will be the mantra that plays in my heart as I go
about my daily life,
And it will be what sings to the hearts of others and
will silently bless all
I encounter as a magnet of **love in the name of
the Father.**

In Thy Name, Blessed Be.

~ ♥ ~

~ Chapter Six ~

The Call of Soul

~ ♥ ~

Love is the only thing that will lead soul out of the darkness and back to its true place in the heart of God. There is no other way.

~ ♥ ~

Sugmad constructed a universe for soul with many paths from which to choose

It is important for soul's evolution to have many life path choices as it makes its way back to the Oceanic Heart of the Beloved One. This insures a well-rounded scope of experience as it meets the many lessons contained within each path chosen. There is never any one way of reaching a spiritual or life goal and the choices are what give soul its character and development. Free will abounds on the road of life and yet there are boundaries that come into effect, brought on by the Guardians of this universe's evolution. If they see that a soul is about to embark on something that will seriously cause imbalance to the whole of life, and is not necessary for karmic development, they will step in and deter that course of action. So what has been thought of as God's "unlimited free will" for human beings **does** have its limits. No person or group of persons will ever be allowed to gravely interfere with the grand scheme of universal destiny. Negative events will still happen in these Lower Worlds because of the cause-and-effect nature of polarities and the need to maintain balance. However, ultimately, all of life is moving forward and many paths are open so that soul will have a multitude of experiences that will open it to Self-Realization and to God-Realization. As soul sees more of itself, God the Father sees more of Itself too.

The Light and Sound emanates and upholds every path of life when Unconditional Love is present

Unconditional love must be the foundation for any true spiritual path that leads soul back to its origins in the Sea of Love and Mercy. Religious doctrines that teach judgment, condemnation and fear of God are devoid of the Light and Sound. The purity of the Essence of God cannot penetrate or find a sympathetic vibration to resonate with in paths of ignorance and hatred. Only when all forms of subjugation and control of others is dropped, and only when fear is replaced with mercy and compassion, can the Light and Sound enter that spiritual path and uplift its members. I will speak briefly here of the Two-Faced religious doctrines that outwardly declare their allegiance to love and compassion for all, mercy and forgiveness, kindness and sharing and brotherhood and charity, while inwardly accumulating and hoarding wealth, greed, avarice and a heavy dose of judgment. The way that one can distinguish the difference between a path of the Light and Sound and the Two-Faced religions is to observe how the leaders and members of any spiritual order treat others when things fall out of alignment with their belief systems. When a person steps outside the "boundaries" of the fold and asks sincere questions, are they met with open-hearted receptivity or are they shunned and rejected? Unconditional love is the deciding factor between a path of the Light and Sound, and all other paths. When the leaders and members conduct themselves with compassion and mercy, you know they are lead by **truth** and **love.**

Anywhere you can find those attributes of the selfless heart you will find the Light and Sound of God.

Soul chooses more direct paths to God as it reincarnates life after life

In this case we can look at soul as a student who is working his or her way up from grade school to high school to college and on to the higher institutions of learning. Nothing in this universe is allowed to remain static; all must move forward in accordance with the Divine Plan. A "complacent" soul or student can fail their courses and have to repeat a class or semester and can even drop out of the entire curriculum, but eventually they will have to return and continue on their learning journey. Each religion is like a specific course of study that teaches unique skills and understanding to the participants. Once the path has been truly absorbed by soul, it must move on to the next and higher class of learning, or it will fall behind and risk stagnation. Each soul intuitively knows when they are ready to move forward, and when that time comes, a master stands by to take their hand and lead them to the next stage of their journey. They may hear of a book or someone may offer to take them to a spiritual class, but each person ready for the next spiritual path will be given the opportunity to move forward. That is the way of love and mercy as God watches over Its children who ascend the ladder of spiritual understanding step-by-step.

The Inner Master will work with spiritual teachers and students of other paths in the attainment of their spiritual goals

In the eyes of the Beloved, we are one great universal family of souls. The feeling of separateness is a function of the human mind and has nothing to do with the true nature of soul. No matter what the spiritual differences may be, all beings are headed toward the same place of reunion with the Divine. The Inner Master works with all souls on all levels of spiritual development toward the attainment of their goals because he or she is the living representative of God's love on Earth. It is his or her responsibility to see that as many souls as possible reach the shores of spiritual enlightenment and freedom. And so he or she works with many different teachers to help them incorporate the Light and Sound into their teachings so that their students will benefit spiritually from the pure waters of love and truth. This is his or her divine purpose on Earth: to release souls from the bondage of the lower planes and set them on the way to the fulfillment of their true purpose and destiny as God-realized beings in the heavenly worlds.

Select spiritual teachers and students of other paths are sitting in the spiritual classes of Ekere Tere and in temples such as Preta Rit on the Etheric Plane

These spiritual classes are like a kind of foreign student exchange program; those who have shown high spiritual potential on other paths are recommended by their teachers to sit in on classes held in Ekere Tere, and in particular, the temple of Preta Rit on the Etheric Plane because of the high learning capability of these students to **absorb and transfer** the knowledge attained and bring it back to their own spiritual paths. Others on those paths will intuitively glean the information that vibrates with a magnetic resonance on the soul bodies of these students and so the information is passed along and shared at an accelerated rate of understanding. The temple of Preta Rit has a unique vibration of wisdom that can easily be absorbed into the consciousness and it is designed to be "transferable" from one soul to another. Most of the temples of learning in Ekere Tere require individual attendance and study, and the wisdom gained is for that soul only, but Preta Rit was created to be a "shared learning laboratory" where one soul can carry that knowledge to a whole body of souls waiting to absorb it into their consciousness. The Masters of Ekere Tere developed this program to speed up the learning process and evolution of those souls who are ready to be **transmitters and receivers** of universal knowledge and wisdom. It is rather a ground- breaking enterprise and is still in the experimental stages. So far, it is showing great success and we are very pleased with its progress!

The Inner Master will re-structure the God seeker's "spiritual signature" once his or her spiritual mission and destiny are discovered

Each soul comes into the world with his or her own spiritual signature that distinguishes them from all other souls in creation. This vibrational signature consists of all they have ever been in all of their lifetimes on Earth and other planets of existence. It represents the resonance of their unique accomplishments, virtues, skills, talents and current level of spiritual development and potential. In the life of each soul there is a turning point of meeting the cause and reason for their current incarnation. This event is similar to the baptism of Jesus when his mission became clear to him in the waters of the River Jordan. At the completion of his baptism, his spiritual signature was changed and he came into the full range of his divine knowledge and understanding. This is what happens when seekers discover their true purpose on Earth; the vibrational structures of their Inner bodies are raised to a higher level so that more Light and Sound can flow through them. They now have the capacity to absorb and reflect more of God's love, compassion and wisdom; and this is what the Inner Master uses to work with each soul as he literally re-configures their spiritual signature to match the higher frequency of the new rate of vibration. This recalibration allows the seeker to unfold at a greater speed with each step taken toward the fulfillment of their mission. It works synergistically so that every effort toward their divine purpose is met and supported by a greater flow of the river of Light and Sound that has been opened within them by the strong, loving hands of the Inner Master.

Each path of life has its own frequency of the Light and Sound

Each path that dedicates itself to the cause of spreading God's love and mercy on Earth will have its own channel to the Light and Sound. This is how the love of God reaches each soul in creation; it is spread through the participants of spiritual paths of merit. The frequency of this channel is determined by the purity of love and truth contained within each path; the greater the message of love, the higher the frequency band of Light and Sound, and the more souls it can reach.

When a path falls out of alignment with love and truth, its channel to the Light and Sound begins to diminish until only a trickle of the Flow of Life remains open. In some cases, a path is completely shut off from the Light and Sound and its growth comes to a grinding halt. This is decided by a group of Masters who work closely with the unseen forces that hold this universe in balance. If a path shows no progress toward goodness and begins to move backward, its flow will be cut off and the rivers of life within it will dry up. When a small trickle is left open, it means that the path maintains hope of turning itself around by the sheer love and devotion of its members. A path can literally be carried by its participants when the leadership fails until new and better leadership can take over. This is the mercy of God's love for His children. He will not allow those who have dedicated themselves with open hearts to a spiritual path to be devastated by the misdeeds of its leaders; He will always leave a window open. Only in the direst cases will a path be shut off forever from the Light and Sound, and even then those participants who have conducted themselves with selfless hearts will be lead to a new path where they can continue their spiritual studies.

Why there is an interchangeable movement of spiritual teachers from one path to another and how this process is like "The Gathering of Many Rivers"

The movement of Teachers from one spiritual path to another is about the distribution of knowledge and wisdom that each Teacher brings with them. A path will become stagnant very quickly when the teachings of only one soul are studied; this is like a small creek winding through the woods and finding no outlet to the sea. When many Teachers come together, they bring with them the Rivers of Wisdom that come from all points of their unique life experiences. These rivers wind through the great terrain of spiritual paths and gather together as one united Flow of Life heading for the Sea of Love and Mercy, where they are absorbed and distributed to the consciousness of humanity and to all life in existence. This is the Gathering of Many Rivers for the advancement of soul toward Self-Realization and God-Realization as he or she makes his or her way from one path to another.

Sugmad (also known as God) required "Love" as the common ground for all balanced paths of life

Love is the foundation of all life and without it there would be nothing but darkness. If love were to be removed from life as we know it, all would fall into a void of suspended animation. There is a grace period given so that Love can return and reanimate creation, but once that period of time has expired, that creation will be destroyed permanently. This is the Mercy of God working through existence; there is always another chance for life to redeem itself, but if there is no indication that goodness will return to one of His worlds, that world will be shut down forever and its souls placed in suspension until He decides to create a new world for them to inhabit.

This is the role of Love in all of life; without it there is no life. And so God required that all spiritual paths designed to lead souls from darkness into light must be maintained by a proper balance of love, truth and compassion; the foremost being that of unconditional love. When a heart is filled with unconditional love, it can hold and transmit that loving energy to all souls within its environment; and the greater the love, the greater the radius of that soul's reach into the world. A path of true spiritual merit is not about reading to a congregation from a holy text, or about preaching to a large television audience about abundance and prosperity. It is about opening the hearts of its participants to understand the meaning and necessity for selfless love in thought and deed. It is about teaching them through spiritual exercises and prayer-song how to access that Love in the realms of God and bring it back to share with others. Love is the only thing that will lead soul out of the darkness and back to its true place in the heart of God. There is no other way.

Humanity is in continual strife, war and pestilence over the difference in religious beliefs

Everyone wants to believe that their religion is the only way back to God and some are willing to fight for that belief. It is one thing to stand behind a belief system and preach it to others. It is another thing to try to force it on others through violence, torture, slavery and murder. Unfortunately, some of the world's great religions **during certain junctures in history** have been twisted into a grotesque mockery of the worship of God through a feverish system of fanaticism, fear, hatred, greed and lust for power. Even in its mildest form, this twisted view of religion and the right to fight for it is what has contributed to the everlasting war and unrest among human beings on Earth. It has fostered pestilence and plagues through the manifestation of unholy thoughts and deeds of the ignorant followers of religious faiths that have fallen from grace.

God does not condone killing in His name, unless it is to protect the innocent. Even then, it must be sanctioned by a loving heart and not one filled with hatred. There is no hatred in God's Kingdom; such lowly emotions belong to the Lower Worlds of darkness and will one day be annihilated when this universal cycle is complete and God closes His eyes to rest before the next universe is created.

Herein is a contemplative prayer for Peace, Love and Greater Brotherhood for Humanity

Heavenly Father, when I seek peace
Let me **give peace** to those in strife;
When I seek love, let me give love
To a motherless child.

When I seek forgiveness, let me **forgive** the one
Who has transgressed against me and left
me brokenhearted.
And when I want comfort, let me find the soul
Whose heart is emptier than mine and give them solace.

Father, make me an instrument of Thy peace,
As Brother Francis has prayed; and let me **be the One**
Who opens the door and shines the light of hope and **giving**
For the weary traveler who seeks rest in
the impending night.

Lead me to understand the stone in my brother's heart;
And let me not fall upon it, but lift it out
And cast it away into the Ocean of Love and **Thy Mercy**,
So that he can feel the lightness of your loving grace.

Father, let there be a star in heaven
For every soul on earth;
And let each star **be the guiding light** for that soul
To find their way back to your loving arms.

Let every person I encounter
Feel the weight of their burdens slip away
By the simple act of a kind word or smile
Given from my Heart, which is **from Your Heart,**
in your Blessed Name.

Here follows a universal contemplative exercise with a mantra that gives peace, love and brotherhood out to the world and to those of the open heart who seek spiritual comfort

1. Imagine in your Third Eye a large, soft blanket of pale blue, pink and lavender; these colors represent peace, love and brotherhood. With this covering you are safe in the arms of Divine Love and Mercy. Wrap yourself comfortably in this blanket and say this mantra three times: **"O-DE-SU-TA-LE-TO"** (pronounced "oh day soo tah lay toh.")

2. Now imagine a room full of people who are hovering in cold and in need of comfort. Go to the center of the room and place your blanket around them and see how it becomes large enough to cover each person in the room with peace, love and comfort. Say **"AH-DE-SU-TA-LE"** (pronounced as "ah day soo tah lay") three times and imagine the blanket now covering the entire world with the feeling of universal brotherhood.

3. Now simply enjoy the feeling of warmth and love as you share this space and time with your brothers and sisters. Stay in this contemplation for 15 minutes and allow the blanket of peace to cover you all with the protection of God's loving grace. Blessed Be.

~ Chapter Seven ~

In the Footsteps of Saints, Prophets, and Holy Men

~ ♥ ~

The heart is where all learning and wisdom takes place and it is not a function of the mind as is generally believed. The mind can only gather facts and information; true knowledge and wisdom occur in the hearts of men and women. .

~ ♥ ~

The common ground of Saints, Prophets and Holy Men and Women (SPH)

The saints, prophets and holy men and women who have walked the earth shared a unique bond of trust and faith in their abilities to carry out their worldly missions. There was never any room for doubt or questioning the wisdom of the God who sent them. In order to carry out a mission of great magnitude for the upliftment of humanity, there must be a feeling of unwavering conviction on the part of the "one who bears the cross," that it can be borne successfully to its divine conclusion. This requires a focus of determination that is not marred by "too much talking." The SPH have mostly been of strong and silent bearing, but also of very cheerful dispositions. This may seem to be a contradiction in terms to be both cheerful and silent, but that is the common characteristic found among the spiritual giants of this world. Silence helps to preserve energy while it builds strength of purpose; cheerfulness opens the hearts of others and creates the light necessary to carry the mission into full activation and completion.

The message of love of SPH is ONE and the same

The underlying message of all the spiritual giants who come to uplift humanity is that of the open, selfless heart and of the recognition of **unity among all souls.** The message is All for One and One for All; it does not teach separation through the ego, but integration of the one true Spirit that connects all living beings. We talk about the "sword" that separates families in the name of God, but it is the sword that cuts the ties of ignorance in the Lower Worlds and releases each participant to find spiritual freedom in an environment of unity with other God seekers whose goal is to return as one great family to their heavenly home in the eternal realms of God. No matter what spiritual path or religion is represented by one of the SPH, there is only one message being conveyed in their words and doctrines because the Father Who Sent Them has only one message for the souls of the world: LOVE ME WITH ALL THY HEART AND LOVE EACH OTHER.

The soul development needed to take the mantle of SPH upon one's shoulders

To take on the mantle of a Saint, Prophet, or Holy Man or Woman, one must have the Inner and Outer fortitude of an Atlas who carries the World upon his shoulders. There is a regiment of "spiritual gymnastics" that is undergone by candidates for SPH training and they have spiritual trainers who will put them through the paces of a workout that entails daily exercises of discipline, endurance, strength, patience and courage. This training is focused upon strengthening the foundation of the Inner bodies so that they are in alignment with the vibratory structures of the worlds in which they will carry out their missions. There are energetic storms in the atmosphere of some worlds that act as a shield against very strong forces for good or evil. One coming in with a divine purpose that will change the societal consciousness of that world must be able to withstand the forces that attempt to keep that consciousness in a state of static non-receptivity. And so the Inner bodies of that SPH candidate must be rigorously trained through tests of strength that are meted out by Masters of the Arts of Universal Change and Progress.

The purpose of any Saint, Prophet, Holy Man or Women or other Spiritual Giant in this world is to bring about **change** and **movement** toward the goals of this Sugmad (God) and to see that Its dream for this universe is brought to completion. The consciousness of many souls in these Lower Worlds has been hardened into rocks of ignorance and must literally be blasted through with the dynamite of spiritual enlightenment that the SPH carry with them. The number one quality of soul development for any member of the SPH is that of **perseverance.** They cannot be swayed or held back by obstacles of any kind and must always find a creative outlet to resolve challenges. The goal to "bring back the flock to the Shepherd" is always before them and is the calling in the stormy winds that can never be unheard or unanswered.

How and why the Archangel Gabriel has been the mentor for the SPH throughout the history of this universe

Archangel Gabriel:

I was part of an early group of souls who were among the first beings created from the heart of this Sugmad (God). I chose to join the Hierarchy of the Angelic Order and worked for many centuries of your time as an angel who ministered to many different forms of life in many different worlds and solar systems. I watched the dinosaurs destroy themselves on your Earth and I helped early mankind to see the first light of divine intuition. It eventually became necessary to send souls who would physically incarnate into the world to minister and walk among men for the enlightenment and redemption of humanity. And so it was left to the Angelic Order to train and mentor those beings who would become one of the Saints, Prophets and Holy Men and Women to walk this Earth in the name of Sugmad to gather the flock of lost souls and lead them back home. As Head of the Angelic Order it has been my privilege and function to oversee the scope of the training of these individuals for their divine tour of duty in the world.

How Archangel Gabriel assesses and studies the Soul Records of those who enter training with him

Archangel Gabriel:

I work closely with Shamus Tabriz in his library on the Causal Plane where the Soul Records of all beings in creation are filed and maintained. Once a soul has applied for training in SPH, his or her records are pulled and carefully reviewed and evaluated. I look for common threads running through that soul's history, which are that of perseverance, fortitude, courage and the ability to interact effectively with others. It is not enough to simply persevere; they must show the demonstrated ability to work with others and influence them for the higher good. For my purpose in overseeing the training for the SPH, the qualities that I look for above all others are those of **leadership** and of **working in harmony with others.** If a soul has shown a leaning toward any kind of tyranny or dictatorship then they are dismissed as candidates. Those who become Saints, Prophets and Holy Men and Women have a Light about them that attracts seekers of truth and divine love. This is what I look for while assessing the Soul Records of potential trainees, the light of strength and humility to lead with wisdom and compassion.

The training behind "The Master Language"

Archangel Gabriel:

Heightening the magnetic resonance of an expressed thought is like tuning a violin; the strings of the energetic signature of the SPH are "tightened" or adjusted until the right notes come forth from the symphony of their Inner consciousness. This method is done in contemplation using highly charged mantras combined with clear visualization techniques. Once these notes are in tune with the higher vibration of Spirit, their resonance attaches to the Universal Soul Consciousness where all language is One and can be understood by all souls in creation. This is known as The Master Language and it is the intuitive communication link between the heart chakras of every being in existence. The Outer words do not matter - they can be in any language or form of writing; what matters is the magnetic resonance attached to the words that go beyond the speaker and beyond the page directly into the heart consciousness of the one who is receiving and "absorbing" those words. What is actually happening is that the symbols representing the thoughts of the teacher are literally absorbed into the consciousness and bypass the mind and ego, going directly into the heart of the student. The heart is where all learning and wisdom takes place and it is not a function of the mind as is generally believed. The mind can only gather facts and information; true knowledge and wisdom occur in the heart of man. The Master Language reaches directly into that place of Inner truth and beauty where there is only love and the state of being in Oneness with all Life.

The SPH have kept their traditional beliefs and teachings vibrant and current with today's times

Master Tremulen:

I would like to join forces with Archangel Gabriel for this response. The methods that are taught to the SPH for the enhancement of their missions on Earth are updated regularly, much like doctors, tax accountants and other professionals who must continually be educated on the newest procedures and information to keep their work on par with the current needs of society. Some of the methods we teach are imbued with an energetic resonance that is self-propelling and expansive. These methods harmonize and integrate with the group and also with the individual consciousness of those who study with the SPH, and as they learn and grow, the teachings expand with them. A good way to explain this would be to compare it to an elastic waistband that stretches with the movement of the body; if the body gains in size, the waistband expands to accommodate the new growth. In other instances, there are classes regularly held in wisdom temples on the Inner planes that not only refresh the SPH on the current state of the world consciousness and times, but also give windows into the future state of events to come. And so the SPH are always "one step ahead" of the game of life and can meet the challenges and needs of the seekers who will come to them for spiritual learning and advancement.

The SPH are the first to defend truth, compassion, justice and equality in world societies

It is the mission of all Saints, Prophets and Holy Men and Women who walk the Earth to preserve the attributes as given above, especially those of **truth** and **compassion** among humanity. Without truth there is no justice, and without compassion there is no equality. The SPH carry the banner of justice for all and are the first to administer love and mercy to the downtrodden masses. Part of their Holy Pledge to Sugmad (God) is to uphold all that is good and gentle in the world. This Holy Pledge is also their cross to bear and their sword to fight to the death for God's righteousness and victory over darkness and ignorance in the realms of man and Spirit. It is this fighting nature, backed by the true and magnetic will of God, which gives the SPH the power to make revolutionary changes in the structure of the social consciousness and human condition. They have the ability to galvanize others toward spiritual greatness by their divinely given magnetic resonance; this is their sacred trust and duty as they fulfill the scope of their worldly missions.

Prophecy is prominent in the Holy Bible within the early Judaic Culture

Life during the biblical times in history was at a turning point. All of humanity was waiting for someone or something to set them free from the bondage and oppression imposed by the Roman government and give them hope, peace, solace and redemption. The time was ripe for prophets who could foresee the future and give assurance to the people that salvation was indeed on the way, and more importantly, **that God had not forsaken them.** This was a time of God-fearing people who believed that God Almighty had turned His back on them, and so they sought out the seers who could return the precious flame of hope to their hearts. Prophecy was a substitute for God to those who felt abandoned by divine love and mercy; it was literally a life-saver to the people of that time and place in early Judea. Even the poorest person would sell his last grains of wheat to consult a seer of merit just to hear a word of encouragement for the future. And so prophecy was as much a way of life in those days as farming, trading, schooling or any other form of life sustainment.

Prophecy was also used as a tool for guidance and decision-making from the lowliest household to the highest rungs of government. Prophets were often considered to be as important as the most eminent political figures because of their ability to see beyond the veil and predict the best course of action for military, social and commercial undertakings. Even the emperor had his own personal seer who was consulted on a daily basis. Prophecy was the way that people in those times could feel a sense of empowerment and bridge the distance between themselves and the Heavenly Father they so longed to embrace.

The blending of prophecy, science, and black magic destroyed the ancient civilizations of Mu, Lemuria and Atlantis

Mu, Lemuria and Atlantis were very advanced civilizations that were meant to herald a gigantic leap in the consciousness of man and take him directly into the God Worlds. Our Sugmad (God) wanted these civilizations to propel the spiritual progress of humanity to the heart and culmination of Its dream for this universe to complete the cycle of births and rebirths and for all souls to return to their true home and claim their heritage as children of God. This was to be the greatest achievement that man would make in the world toward his quest to be reunited with the Father of All and to take his rightful place in the Kingdom of Heaven. That is how important were these lands of Lemuria (also known as Mu) and Atlantis, a sister-land to Mu. And so they were given the Holy Secrets of Eternal Truths to be used like a blast of spiritual dynamite for mankind to break through the restrictions of the Lower Worlds and see the doors of heaven open to spiritual freedom, wisdom, knowledge and understanding.

Special souls were selected to incarnate into these civilizations; they were highly trained in the use of the divine secrets, which would not only illuminate the human consciousness, but would also change and reconfigure its very structure so the speed of advancement would accelerate a thousand-fold. Some of these souls were Masters and members of the SPH who had walked the Earth many times. Some of them came from other planets and solar systems to work with mankind toward the goal of its spiritual progress. All were hand picked by the Grand Council so that only those of the highest moral and spiritual fiber would be allowed access to secrets that had never before been uncovered in this world. And so these masterful souls from all across the universes in creation came to incarnate on the continent of Mu, which existed in the Pacific Ocean and included sections now known as Africa and southern Asia. They used the secrets of life to open the minds and hearts of souls and for great scientific and technological achievement. There was great spiritual evolution, harmony and enjoyment of life because of their highly advanced technology, which included the harnessing of crystal energy for use in healing, travel, light, heating and a myriad of other applications. This was a telepathic race of people with fully developed psychic abilities that lived in balance with nature and science for many centuries.

But over time, there came to be a host of black magicians who wanted to use the powerful sources of energy from crystals and psychic storms of the Astral Planes to further their own causes for wealth, power, and dominion over the Earth. Their powerful sorcery harnessed the precious secrets of science and prophecy and perverted them to unleash forces that were never meant to exist in the physical world. These forces upset the natural balance of earth, air and water; they confused the human consciousness and even set it in backward motion - all for the lust and thrill of believing they could do whatever they wanted with the powers at their control - so they could become gods in their own lifetime, but they were gravely mistaken. The forces they had set in motion took on a life of their own, gaining momentum like an avalanche of destruction and chaos. The very essence of nature was shaken to the core and aroused to a raging fury that resulted in the cataclysmic volcanic eruptions that destroyed the entire continent of Lemuria and Mu. Its sister land of Atlantis was also affected by the scourge of black magic and was also destroyed by the powerful earthquakes and tidal waves that were set off by unnatural sources such as the deliberate misuse of crystal power.

This is similar to the fate that awaits mankind today with the dangers of nuclear energy. *The Masters who oversee this universe are working closely with Beings who were sent to this Earth to restore and restructure the native balance and harmony within the hearts of men* and within all nature in order to avoid the catastrophe that looms ahead and to ensure that it does not happen again. Hope rests within the understanding that we can learn from our past mistakes.

Forthcoming changes to our planet in the next five thousand years

Voices of Future Living Sehaji Masters:

By the year 7,000 AD a new race of beings will have inhabited the Earth and integrated their culture into life on this planet. These are the "lost brothers" whose return at the end of this century has been foretold in other dialogues in the writings of Dan Rin. They are a race very similar to humans in physical and emotional structure; they have compassion, industry, and are of a peace seeking nature.

Paramitas, the Gathering of Many Rivers

By 3100 they will have completely merged their species with the human race so that only one dominant race will exist on Earth. These are the reincarnated souls of the lost civilizations of Lemuria and Atlantis who once thrived on this planet. They carry with them the secret teachings and advanced technology of their once great culture that will be revived on Earth for a second renaissance of the golden age of man. This time, the shadow of black magic will not darken the sky of the new world and its inhabitants will be allowed to finish what was started in the great evolution of souls so many eons ago.

There will be flying machines for interplanetary travel that are made up of light molecules of energy. The bodies of travelers will be able to "disintegrate" to fit the vibration necessary for time travel as these machines will cross not only distance but time itself. There will be no such thing as automobiles and gasoline, as they will have become obsolete along with the dinosaurs. Everything in the new world will center on the use of light energy from crystals and other precious minerals and stones. All healing will be done with auric energy techniques that do not require invasion of the body with cutting instruments. These techniques will remove mental, emotional, causal and etheric blockages from the Inner bodies that will allow the physical body to heal itself naturally by the use of Sound and Light. Much healing will be done with sound instruments held closely over afflicted areas of the body. The proper sounds, such as notes and harmonics, will be designed on a unique and individual basis by those who are highly trained in this art to support the magnetic signature of the patient and restore them to balance. There will be no more hospitals and HMO's; they will be rusting in the scrap yard along with cars and dinosaurs.

The condition of the Earth itself will be vastly changed because of the shifting of the axis in the middle of the next century. Lands that were long submerged will rise from the sea and toxic lands damaged by modern technology will disappear into Neptune's Kingdom. The newly risen lands will bring forth flora and fauna not seen in this world for thousands of centuries. There will be new plant species for botanists to enjoy and new fruits, vegetables, grains and legumes for the culinary adventurers.

The main forms of entertainment will still be "movies," but the way they are produced and seen will be of a much grander nature, as they will take on the pictures stored in the Akashic Records of the Astral Plane and literally "show" people their past and future lives. Movies based on real experiences will never be truer and "reality entertainment" will take on new meaning!

As for the spiritual nature of soul in the coming millennia, with the removal of black magic and the vibrations of heavy energies that were trapped in the Earth now submerged into the sea, there will be a startling shift forward in all areas of spiritual advancement from clairvoyance and telepathy to bilocation, manifestation, interplanetary soul movement, and some that cannot yet be explained in these writings. Compassion and love will be the most dominant of the "human" emotions, as life will be of such quality that all beings will be able to enjoy a higher standard of living and there will be no reason for greed and hatred.

Most communication will be done by telepathy by the year 4,000. And there will be computers that read minds and transfer the information to other computers that are designed to receive and transmit telepathic information that can be transcribed into documents for reading and filing. There will be no more schools and education as we know it today; all learning will be done through telepathic methods that cannot be described here, as the mental body of man cannot receive or make sense of it at this stage of its development.

There is a brave new world coming this way with golden opportunities for the advancement of soul in the Renaissance of Humanity on Earth. It will begin with the return of the Brotherhood of Atlanteans and Lemurians who will replenish this planet and restore it to its former splendor, power and magnificence at the end of this century. That will truly be the "dawning of a new age" of spiritual growth, brotherly love, and the understanding of how to use natural resources to gain tremendous technological achievement in healing, education, industry and travel. It will be the time of soul's greatest journey yet to the center of the universe and the heart of the Eternal One.

Herein follows a contemplative exercise that will give our participants insight into their own potential futures

1. The heart is an oasis from suffering and strife; imagine in your Third Eye that your heart is an island floating on a deep blue sea of possibilities and potential futures.

2. Sit down on the warm sand and write down a question about your future; it can be anything from asking about a romantic partner or a new job; or looking ten, twenty, thirty years ahead and more to ask for a window into the world to come and what will be your role in it. You can also ask about future lifetimes yet to be lived. Anything goes.

3. Write it down, then place the piece of paper in a clear glass bottle and toss it as far as you can into the sea. As the bottle leaves your hand, say this mantra: **"O-SE-TU-SAVA-TE"** (pronounced "oh say too sahvah tay.") It is only necessary to say it once.

4. Relax on the sand; lie on your back and watch the sky overhead. It is clear blue, but notice that wisps of clouds are forming in the center of the sky, making words and pictures. Just watch for the message they have for you in response to your question. It could be a single word, or a full length movie with color and sound. Again, anything goes. Experiment with this exercise and have fun!

~ ♥ ~

Paramitas, the Gathering of Many Rivers

~ Chapter Eight ~

The Court of Sat Nam

~ ♥ ~

The Fifth Plane is the jewel that shines on the left hand of God; it is the bearer of the promise of eternal love, devotion and joy that waits for those who will take the vow of holy union with the Beloved One.

~ ♥ ~

The Grand Council chose Sat Nam as the Guardian of the Fifth Plane, known as the Soul Plane

The United Voices of the Grand Council:

The great Sat Nam was once a soul of great merit in this universe's beginnings and an Overseer of a region in the outlands of the universe known as Tirahan. This was a port where flying ships from all parts of intergalactic space would stop to acclimate to the atmosphere of this solar system and pass inspection before entering that planetary realm. Sat Nam's responsibility was to guarantee the safety of the space travelers and their vessels as they made their way from one star system to another. He made sure that all beings who entered the domain of the lower physical universe were well-protected and of good intentions. He was known as an Ambassador of the Light and Sound and he fulfilled his duties with dignity, forcefulness and integrity. No one dared to cross this venerable being in the execution of his work and he gained the respect and admiration of the Holy Order of Ancient Ones of the Grand Council who gave their report directly to the Sugmad Itself. And so when it came time to choose a Ruler for the Worlds below the Great Divide, the Sugmad appointed this Holy Being, whom It named Sat Nam, to reign over Its kingdom and represent Its interests as a direct manifestation of Itself. Sat Nam was given new life in a ceremony similar to baptism, in which an aspect of the Sugmad as the Holy Spirit joined with the soul of Sat Nam and allowed Sat Nam to fully come into His powers as the God of the Fifth Plane and emerge as the first true manifestation of the Supreme God of the Universe.

Sat Nam's Court is an ideal meeting place for the Grey, White and Beige Robe Hierarchies to confer and deliberate with each other

These Robed Orders are the top three hierarchies in the Kingdom of Sugmad (God). Their territories intersect that of Sat Nam and their interests and responsibilities coincide with the Lord of the Five Planes below the Great Divide. All that is discussed in the Court of Sat Nam has to do with the workings and goings on from the Soul Plane down to the Physical Plane. Each hierarchy is responsible for a different section of life within the vastness of these planes of existence and they gather at a common meeting ground to discuss their findings and issues; concerns, solutions and directives; and administrative applications. The Court of Sat Nam is situated in an ideal place for these meetings because of its accessibility to both the Higher and Lower Worlds; it is like an ambassadorship to the Light and Dark forces that maintains all balance in the worlds of duality and those pure energies that uphold the highest realms of Spirit. It is also a "neutral" place for the gathering of different vibratory energies where they will not clash with each other, but blend into a harmonious group understanding, so much can be worked out and accomplished; and the various interests acknowledged and satisfied.

Soul Records of God seekers who are established on the Soul Plane

Dan Rin:

After the Fifth Initiation, the causal records of God seekers who have reached the Soul Plane are transferred from the Causal Plane to Sat Nam's keeping in order to prevent psychics and others with ill intent from examining the past lives of those in

the God Worlds; it is a security issue. Soul Records have to be maintained on the Causal Plane until the God seeker's vibration can support and accommodate the heights of the God Worlds.

I wish to add here that Shamus Tabriz has done an excellent job in overseeing and protecting the Soul Records of those God seekers who have yet to reach the summit of the Soul Plane. His work is invaluable in the forward movement of humanity as it seeks to understand itself from its past life history. He understands the need to protect the records of those souls who continue to move higher into the God Worlds; the higher they go, the stronger is the need for security. For instance, the records of the Living Master are not kept with Sat Nam, but higher, in a place that is completely inaccessible to any soul but the One who is guarding and maintaining them for him. This is because there are many "red soldiers" from the battlements of deep, inner space who would love to tear the Living Master apart and reveal his innermost secrets to opposing forces in the universe who are always plotting the destruction of the divine plans of this Sugmad (God), so that the Dark Lords they serve can overtake this Universe and populate it with their own kind and serve their own interests. Many would love to conquer this universal enterprise of God Almighty and create their own worlds for their own amusement, self-aggrandizement, and power. It all starts with the right "information" that can be stolen from the Soul Records of Saints and Masters and those Spiritual Giants whose names have never been spoken. This is why there is a Hierarchy in the keeping of Soul Records in the universe of this Sugmad. The security of these records is **inviolable and absolute.**

The function of the sanskaras

The purpose and function of the *sanskaras* (the magnetic energy wrappings around the body) is to identify each soul by its own magnetic signature. This consists of the accumulation of energy behind each experience of that soul's many lifetimes on all planes of reality. Each experience creates an energy pattern that forms a circle around the soul's lower bodies and can easily be seen and read by Spiritual Travelers of the Inner realms. These energetic patterns or "sanskaras" tell the complete story of that soul's history and of its current state of spiritual development. They bind souls to their experiences and keep them wrapped within the soul memories or "engrams" attached to those experiences. A soul deeply wrapped within the influence of the sanskaras can be induced to repeat the same experiences over and over again, forming what is known as "karmic loops." The spell of the engrams behind these loops creates a tremendous temptation for soul and can only be broken by the presence of a Spiritual Master who is fully anchored in the Soul Planes and has the wisdom, knowledge, and experience to free God seekers from the bondage of their sanskaras through the use of highly charged mantras and spiritual exercises. Only then can souls free themselves from the wrappings of the sanskaras and continue their journeys into the true worlds of Spirit.

Soul's establishment in Sat Nam's Court

The sanskaras are a feature of the lower worlds of duality where souls have garnered experiences on their way back to the God Worlds. Once a God seeker has reached solid footing on the Fifth Plane, his or her consciousness has been raised to a vibratory level that literally breaks through the lower, slower vibration of the sanskaras and they begin to lose their grasp and drop away.

This does not happen immediately, but once a soul has crossed the threshold into the first plane of the higher realms and set foot in the Court of Sat Nam, that soul is given the "seal of recognition" which is like an emblem that appears in their magnetic signature and resonates at an increased level of vibration that affects the sanskaras and allows them to dissipate and disappear at a rate that suits the consciousness of that individual soul. It would be too much of a shock for soul if the sanskaras were to drop away all at once. Thus, the stamp of Sat Nam gives this process the proper method of unfoldment and completion so that all stays in alignment for the spiritual progress of the God seeker.

The Fifth Plane has been viewed as a "resting place" for souls before they continue their journey into the God Worlds

The Fifth Plane is viewed by the Masters of Olde as the eternal doorway between the worlds of illusion and the worlds of Spirit. This is the sacred threshold all souls must cross before they can begin their true journey into the God Worlds. It takes most souls several millennia before they have been prepared by the trials of their worldly existence to once again taste the sweet nectar of salvation and the restoration of their true heritage and memories as children of God. Even one lifetime in the lower worlds of duality can take its toll on a human being and sixty years of life served in the Physical Plane is worth one hundred fifty years of rest in the spiritual realms. By the time souls have reached the point where they are ready to leave the worlds of duality forever, they have endured thousands of years of tests and challenges. They must be restored and rejuvenated in the sanctuary of the first true home of Spirit on the Fifth Plane under the rule of the great Sat Nam. This is where all souls come to rest before continuing their journey to the higher worlds of

God that beckon with the glory of mysteries yet to be uncovered and savored. The Fifth Plane is the jewel that shines on the left hand of God; it is the bearer of the promise of eternal love, devotion and joy that waits for those who will take the vow of holy union with the Beloved One. It is the honeymoon suite where souls find their first taste of pure bliss before they embark on their new lives as true companions of God.

The Fifth Circle of Initiation brings changes to the God seeker's Life Contract

The Fifth Circle of Initiation is the true "crossing over" into the worlds of God. Life as it was known in the physical planes will be forever left behind. This occurrence requires an increased rate of vibration within the God seeker's consciousness so that all dross can be cleared away and what remains of their former life will be transformed in order to accommodate the expansion of their consciousness. A consequence of this event is the loss of relationships with those who cannot adjust to the higher vibration within the God seeker. They attempt to pull him back to his former self and get very angry and upset with the threat of losing the familiar connection they previously had with their loved one. When this occurs within a marital relationship, divorce is often the result. The Contract between the two souls is broken; not only in the physical reality, but also on the spiritual side where the Initiate of the Fifth Circle and above has appealed to the Lords of Karma to release them from their binding Contract with that other soul or spouse who would hold him or her back from their spiritual destiny. And yet when all matters are said and done, there is nothing more powerful on Earth than the love we developed and have for those we love.

Life Contracts are written to be quite fluid with the movement of souls as they make their way back to the worlds of Spirit. When the Lords of Karma see that an advanced soul has fulfilled an aspect of his or her Contract that would have continued to play out indefinitely, they will amend it accordingly. The Law of Economy applies to all souls who have crossed into the Fifth Circle in that they are allowed to "jump the groove" and move on to the next song or leave the album entirely and start a new one when staying with the same old song would seriously hinder their progress. When one soul is kept behind, all souls are thus impeded from moving forward. There is a "domino effect" in the universal structure of life - all beings are affected by the fall of even one soul. This is why careful consideration is given to the Life Contracts of those souls who have reached the first pinnacle of success in their quest for spiritual freedom and evolvement. Every effort is made to insure that the Contract expands along with the consciousness of the soul who has reached the Fifth Plane of Heaven and above. Nothing and no one can stand in the way of God's plan and dream for all souls who are catching their first glimpse of His Magnificent Face in the Court of Sat Nam. And so the Fifth Initiation marks the turning point for souls with the recalibration of their energetic life code or signature and the revision of their Life Contracts to stay in alignment with their continued journeys into the higher realms of the first true worlds of Spirit.

The God Power Individuates Itself into those souls already established in Sat Nam's Court

The God Power is funneled in through the crown chakra at the top of the head of the individual and becomes charged when the Seal of Recognition is bestowed upon them by Sat Nam. Once the power is thus activated the lower bodies begin to vibrate at an increased level that affects the sanskaras; they loosen their hold and begin to slowly dissolve. This process changes the "engrammatic" patterns or "soul memories" within the emotional and mental bodies where the seat of perception has its foundation. The individual begins to perceive all experiences at the soul level and this in turn affects how they react and relate to life. As they see from this higher vantage point their behavior changes accordingly and old personality traits that do not resonate with this higher perception begin to drop away. And so friends of that soul who is charged by the God Power start to notice a change in their personality; the person they knew no longer indulges in the same kind of activities and conversations as before. For instance, they no longer find gossip to be entertaining because they see the highest aspects of others rather than relishing their weaknesses. This makes them no fun for the old friends who want them to drink, gossip, and make merry. One who is charged with the God Power seeks out those people who will reflect and harmonize with their enlightened state of consciousness and enjoy the challenge of seeking the truth behind all illusion. It can be a very long and lonely road, for there will be fewer and fewer companions who will stay by their side, but it is a deeply rewarding journey that does not dead-end into aimless self-indulgence; it takes the God seeker beyond all he or she has ever known and onto the great and glorious highways to spiritual growth, discovery and freedom.

Sugmad's Highest Good

The residents of the Fifth Plane must wear the mantle of selflessness in all they do. They learn to do good works purely for their own sake. Loving the work is the key to understanding how to utilize their initiation for the Sugmad's highest good. There should be no thought that "this work will please God and raise me in His estimation." Good works done with selfish or self-serving intentions have no value in the eyes of God. A man who gives food to a hungry person with no thought other than to relieve their suffering is worth far more to Divine Love than one who provides a banquet to thousands and basks in the glory of their gratitude and acknowledgment. St. Francis of Assisi said,

"Do all in the name and for the love of the One who died on the Cross; when He smiles upon you, that is your reward." His idea is a simple one, yet very profound - bring the love of Spirit into all you do; take God with you in all of your ways, but above all, bring your selfless heart to the table of Divine Giving; there is no requirement to even serve God Itself, but only that you come from a pure and selfless heart in your offering of service to the world.

Secrets behind the Power of Theta

The Power of Theta has the ability to completely restructure the electrical makeup of the human body through the use of sounds that readjust the brainwave patterns. This is similar to sound therapy, but goes much deeper than what is currently being used. There are ways to tap into the pure, harmonic energies that come directly from the Fountain of the Sound Current. That is to say, they come directly from Sugmad or God Itself. **The origin of the sound is what makes the crucial and most beneficial difference;** it is not caused by a physical instrument, but comes from the Inner planes and is channeled by one who is trained and skilled in the art of **inner sound transference.** This practitioner literally channels the pure strains of the Voice of the Universe down into the human energy field where it is distributed through the electrical grids of the four invisible bodies and then through the chakras of the physical shell.

This is a highly skilled art and is used by only a very few souls who have been able to truly understand and master its use. The Teacher who instructs in this specialized health method is called Lo-Tan and he has worked for 10,000 years as overseer of the Temple of the Lords of Karma. Lo-Tan is a quiet and mysterious being who prefers to do his work outside of prying eyes and questions. When he comes forth he is escorted by a legion of monks who wear brown hooded robes. These are his assistants who have pledged and proven their loyalty to the secrecy and sacredness of his work with the Power of Theta. Master Lo-Tan is highly revered among the Lords of Karma and this work is closely associated with their interests and domain because of its ability to strongly affect the balance of karmic distribution and resolution.

At present, there are very few human beings who know how to use this power to heal, but the numbers will soon be growing, especially at the beginning of the year 2012 when a new wave of energy will sweep down from the God Worlds into the Lower Worlds for a periodic cleansing of old and dead energy. The influx of energy is like removing layers of dirt from the floor to allow the natural finish to shine forth once again. When this happens, there will be a renewal of natural and holistic healing practices and many people will benefit from the use of the Theta Power for the healing of every kind of human ailment from arthritis to cancer. The Lords of Karma have given their permission to "bump" the traditional healing methods of synthetic drugs, invasive surgeries and health organizations off the medical roadmap and merge them with the natural healing ability of the Sound Current as it is applied to the human brain through the use of Theta Power. Theta is the level of brainwave activity that occurs just before sleep and just upon awakening. It is the most pure and receptive time for the human brain and spiritual consciousness to accept and utilize the Sound Current for the optimal healing of the body on all levels – physical, astral, causal, mental and etheric.

The Theta Power is a blending of the cooperative work between the physical and the spiritual consciousnesses; one cannot succeed without the full participation of the other. It is a highly synergistic method of healing that is all-encompassing in scope and results. In the next few years to come, we happily anticipate the miraculous Power of Theta as it begins its true journey into the Lower Worlds of mankind to completely change the face of medical practice as we know it today. This is a very exciting time for humanity!

Special words from Dan Rin

I would like to add here that the Power of Theta has been in the world for many centuries. Moses, Jesus, Ezekiel and many early prophets understood this power but they could not fully utilize it because of its potential to interfere with the laws of balance and karma. Permission is required from the Lords of Karma to use the Theta method of healing. This power has yet to be fully harnessed to its maximum potential, but once fully understood, it can be used by soul to adjust the brainwave pattern to heal what ails the human body and return it to its natural electrical state of being.

Lo-Tan and the power of Theta

Lo-Tan:

This is an unusual process in that the souls who are ready for this training are not selected from the outside but from "within." In other words, they know that this is their calling and at the appointed time, they simply come to me and volunteer their services. They receive a strong Inner signal that this is their next step, to learn the art of Theta Power healing and I can hear them coming before they knock upon the door to my inner sanctuary. As they approach, the door swings open and we begin the training process. You may wonder if any who "volunteer" in this way have made a mistake and are turned away. This has never happened yet, because the signal comes from soul and he or she simply knows his or her destiny as a healer of this magnitude. I do ask that the Lords of Karma sit in on my first meeting with a volunteer to scan his or her energy field and confirm that they are who they say they are, and that they are indeed qualified for my training. And then we proceed.

The training consists of a series of tests that gauge the ability to send and receive healing energy from the Sound Current. This is central to using the Theta Power. It is the Sound Current that controls the brainwave signals sent to the body; and the body responds by realigning its electrical patterns to work in harmony with the Inner power grids and chakras and restore itself to optimal functioning and health. Harnessing the Sound Current to work through the body has been the quest of scholars and scientists throughout history. Some of them have made significant progress in using brainwave technology to heal the body but were mostly thwarted in the effort to bring their work to success and distribution by forces of the negative side who want to keep mankind in a constant loop of struggle with pain and suffering. The successful use of brainwave and/or Theta Power for **worldwide** healing will completely change the health practices of the world. Simply put, there would a critical change to the dynamics of the medical professional's job description and our use of hospitals; there would only be my health practitioners doing their work on behalf of the Lords of Karma, the Nine Silent Ones, and the Great Almighty Sugmad. It has always been the Sugmad's wish to have the heavy shroud of illness lifted from the back of mankind; it is not meant that man should suffer in this way. He has brought it upon himself by losing his natural connection with the Sound Current that the Almighty Father gave to His children to use as their universal salvation, redemption and passage back to their true and divine heritage. The Sound Current is the signal to follow for health and wellbeing and was at one time a part of the medulla oblongata but the connection has since been destroyed by the habitual expression of negative thoughts and emotions and by the abuse of drugs, narcotics and alcohol. The connection can however be restored through the proper reintroduction of the Theta Power current by a skilled practitioner. I see this happening within the next ten years and I have dedicated a great part of my mission to the success of this magnificent healing project brought forth from the holy realms of Heaven Itself. That is all.

Here follows a contemplative exercise that will give the God seeker entry and an understanding of what awaits them in Sat Nam's Court

1. Imagine you are comfortably riding on a huge elephant; you are securely seated in a chair strapped to the elephant's back and are moving steadily toward a monumental gate with two pillars at either side at the tops of which are torches burning with fire that reach far into the sky. There is the sound of drums coming from beyond the gate that have a rhythmic, soothing beat. They beat with the rhythm of your own heart. As you approach the gates, they begin to slowly swing open and you can begin to see what lies in wait.

2. Pass through the gates and say this mantra three times: **"SULAY-TA-OVAY-TIKA.**

3. You are now being greeted by two servants in white clothing and white turbans. They help you down from the elephant's back and lead you to an altar that sits in the open space of a massive garden of tropical plants and flowers. There they leave you in silence and solitude.

4. Soon, a light glows from the center of the altar and within this light a face begins to appear, or it may just be two eyes that shine from within the light. Look into the eyes and know that you are communing with a reflection of the great Sat Nam Himself. Simply gaze into the eyes

of this holy manifestation of God and allow whatever wisdom, knowledge or information He has for you to enter into you, through your heart. Blessed Be.

~ Chapter Nine ~

The Grand Council

~ ♥ ~

We wish to bring back peace, harmony and goodwill on Earth and this begins with the Inner and Outer – the spiritual, mental, emotional and physical health of mankind.

~ ♥ ~

The Sugmad constructed the Grand Council

The Great Sage Milarepa will take the helm on this inquiry:

The Grand Council was constructed by Sugmad to give a body of law, order and structure to the evolving and untamed universal frontier. Every star, planet, sun and moon was given a name by the one and only Holy Father and nothing was left to chance as the firmament of the heavens took shape and substance. The Grand Council was there when Sugmad closed Its eyes and dreamed of soul as a way of seeing, knowing and loving Itself. The first souls to emerge into being were blessed by the Grand Council and closely monitored to follow their progress in the God Worlds and later into the Lower Worlds. All of the planes of existence from the highest realms to the lowest rungs were created under the supervision of the Grand Council. There is nothing in the entire Creation of Sugmad that does not fall within their jurisdiction. Their holy presence is what gives this universe its laws and balance, and it is what keeps it from descending into chaos and destruction.

The Grand Council is comprised of Olden Ones of a Holy Order that precedes the dream of Sugmad. They were there while the Sugmad rested and they originate from Its Holy Father of Fathers, the Nameless One that gave them life and sustenance from the spark of Its Own Being. The first members of the Grand Council were three souls who formed the Trinity of Father (Nameless One), Son (Sugmad) and Holy Ghost (Spirit). They reported directly to Sugmad even though they had the same aspects of Being and were likened as to Its "Brothers." As a Trinity they formed a balance of power that surrounded and upheld the Inner and Outer workings of this Universe. The head of this Holy Trio of the Grand Council was a soul named Therion. This being has no age or physical description, but will often take on the visage of a non-human form that represents the twin aspects of God's expression in the Lower Worlds, that of the Light and Sound. And so this early Trinity of the Grand Council maintained the entire functioning of the Universe for eleven billion years, and as the Universe expanded, new members were added to accommodate the growth of life and creation. The Grand Council now stands at twelve members which has been their number for the past two thousand centuries of your time. I have been the Head of this Order of the Sehaji for all of that time. It has been my great honor, reward, pleasure and distinction to serve All Life in this capacity. And I have watched many worlds come and go. The current world under the guidance and mission of Dan Rin is the most exciting and promising of all that has gone before. This Living Master is the most fearless and honorable soul to ever hold the Rod of Power. We of the Grand Council stand vigilantly by his side and together will turn the tide of the Lower Worlds from the murky depths of darkness to the illumined shores of spiritual emancipation, joy, love, power and Reunion with God for All souls.

Milarepa was chosen as Head of the Council

Master Milarepa:

I was chosen because of my deep affinity for the spiritual and universal laws that uphold justice, fairness, virtue, compassion, righteousness, benevolence, trust, honor and duty; and love and service toward all Life. My quest has always been to be at the helm of progress, emancipation, understanding and brotherhood among all souls in the worlds of Sugmad. I descend from the lineage of the White Robed Order and rode with the White Brotherhood alongside great souls like Milati, Socrates, Plato, Aristotle, Tindor Saki and Archangel Gabriel. I am directly linked to one of the First Three Members of the Original Grand Council and have that soul's memories within my magnetic resonance. Everything that has ever transpired since this universe was created is contained within my awareness and understanding. I am without question the most versed and qualified soul to stand at the Head of the current Grand Council that oversees the unfoldment of all life in all the worlds of Sugmad and beyond, but I do not stand alone, for there are my Brothers of the Council without whom I cannot fully execute and complete my duties. This is a group effort of highly exceptional Spiritual Masters working together for the good of the whole of all creation, but as with any ship sailing the golden seas, there can be only one captain and I am that one who stands ready at the helm to steer this vessel steadily toward the Best-Laid Plans of the Sugmad that I serve.

The other Council Members were chosen by virtue of the various strengths, experience and expertise that each one brings into the fold. They come from all areas of the universe and beyond into other realities past space and time. Some have come from the future and some have never known a human form; for instance, Kadmon and Milati are not human, though they take on a familiar form that can be identified and understood for the sake of communication. There are some Masters who stay for varying durations of time but there are always twelve in Council and in discussion. We sometimes have visiting dignitaries who sit in to listen and the conversation is always of a serious nature. These conferences involve mostly Masters of the universe who visit and the Silent Nine. Many of the Olden Ones of this universe come to speak before us; Jesus came before us just after he translated from his earthly mission. The Living Master sits down with us once weekly and sometimes more, depending on the need.

The Grand Council and planetary Best-Laid Plans

Master Milarepa:

There is a blueprint of plans for this universe that entails the whole of humanity as it makes its way back to the Godhead. Within these overall plans are micro-plans for every year, day and down to the minute of all that will transpire for the next four billion years. The Grand Council meets with the Silent Nine and the Lords of Karma on a regular basis to discuss and implement these ever-evolving plans. There is much overlay involved in maintaining these plans to keep them fresh and up-to-date with current needs. They originate from the heart of Sugmad who makes Its wishes known to the Silent Nine, and they in turn inform the Grand Council. Then the Lords of Karma are called into the discussion and the plans begin to take shape.

Much is in store for this universe and for its Mother Earth in this current century, including the overhaul of the military forces that have dominated this physical world, especially that of the United States, China, Russia, England and areas of the Middle East. We see the military as having the greatest influence on the lifespan of the Earth's inner resources, of its heart and spirit. The Earth cannot survive endless wars, invasions and occupations of its lands and people. Mother Earth cries for her children and for her body and has been in great pain and suffering for many centuries. This Earth is a living soul, as are all other souls in creation, and the fighting upon her flesh must stop now. So we are creating a plan that will abolish the way wars are currently fought and even abolish the need for them. This new wave of peace will come in with the return of the Lost Brothers from Mu and Lemuria as they re-take and re-populate the soil of this earth at the end of this century. This will herald a new age of peace and brotherhood among men, but not without its strife as the new legs of the calf must become strong and steady to carry the weight and might of the bull. This wave of change must fight its way to growth and survival, but once it does, it will lead the herd to new and greener pastures.

So that is one of the major plans that will have a trickle down effect on many other aspects of life in the Lower Worlds. We of the Grand Council also want to change the way medicine is practiced and so the resurgence of Theta Power healing will take its true place in the world of humans as the way of keeping the physical body in alignment with its natural electrical balance. We wish to bring back peace, harmony and goodwill on Earth and this begins with the Inner and Outer – the spiritual, mental, emotional and physical health of mankind. **Illness has been the root cause of all war and strife on earth** – not the greed for wealth, land and power, or the struggle for domination among religious groups; these are only the effects from the true cause of war which is **the lack of inner peace and physical well-being in mankind.** Much harm has been done by those in positions of leadership who are out of balance in body, mind and spirit. There must be a return to health and well-being in the body, mind and heart of humanity. And so these are two of the Best-Laid Plans that we of the Grand Council, the Silent Nine and the Lords of Karma are currently and vigilantly working on to insure the survival of the human race, of Mother Earth, and of this grand and magnificent Universe.

Africa's Renaissance and Best-Laid Plans

Master Milarepa:

The role of Africa in the Best-Laid Plans for the Lower Worlds is to unify the four corners of the globe – America, Africa, Europe and Asia. Africa is the unifying force that holds the four continents together geographically and spiritually by virtue of its role as Mother and Nurturer. It is the home and hearth of the Earth. Sugmad bestowed the African continent with the heart in the body of the physical worlds – it is the pulse to which all on this Earth follows in rhythm and is the place from which the blood of life flows to all other parts of the world. The heartbeat of Africa has been slowed to a coma by ten thousand years of black magic practiced on her lands. Her renaissance is the resurrection of the heartbeat of Mother Earth as it is cleansed of clogged arteries and the blood of life opens wide and free once again to flow to all parts of the globe.

This resurgence of energy marks the beginning of a new lease on life for this Earth and its inhabitants, and it paves the way for the return of the Kulgars – the race of beings that is returning to this planet at the end of this century. These events follow in alignment with Best-Laid Plans; the resurrection of the heart of Africa is the catalyst for the fulfillment of these sacred plans which have been in the making for some five million years.

The Way of Truth Eternal, Book I has given word and form to the magnetic resonance of these Plans. It has given them a voice on Earth and is the grounding force for their physical manifestation and implementation. All plans begin as energetic signatures in the high planes of Sugmad. They are then given form and substance by a vehicle in the physical realms such as a book through which they can be harnessed and energized by one who has the power of the Holy Spirit in manifestation, such as the Living Master. This is an example of the sequence of activity through which Best-Laid Plans are brought forth and realized in the Lower Worlds.

The cycle of this planet's regeneration

The regeneration of planet Earth cannot be accomplished without the participation of its inhabitants, especially those endowed with the Light and Sound of God – the stronger the flow of God power they carry, the greater is their ability to lift this planet into rejuvenation and trigger its regenerative properties. All souls on Earth have the capacity to uplift the planet, but most are asleep to their connection to the divine flow of Spirit. And so it is left to the Initiates of the Light and Sound to carry Earth on waves of HU to the harmonic reconstruction of its many layers of consciousness. This is a massive group effort to restore this planet to health and never before have there been so many children of the Light and Sound upon its holy lands and waters. All who inhabit the Earth are connected on a soul level to the planet by invisible cords of light; similar to the "silver cord" that connects soul to its physical vehicle. While they live on this Earth, the purity or non-purity of their consciousness affects Earth for good or bad. Most souls here are at a very low level of consciousness and do not understand their relationship as children of Mother Earth. They have abused, neglected and destroyed her lands and natural resources. And so it is up to the mature brothers and sisters initiated into the Light and Sound to rebalance, re-energize, re-harmonize and re-generate the Earth to its former state of well being. The Earth has no physical aging process and can be fully restored to youthfulness by the good works of its inhabitants. They in turn also benefit from this rejuvenation process within their own bodies and experience increased vitality and longevity. So it is a win-win situation for all concerned!

The challenges of vanity and ego

Vanity and ego are two sides of the same mirror - they reflect back to the viewer a double-image of that which keeps humanity trapped in the Lower Worlds. Vanity is the aspect of ego that represents the lost soul who wanders aimlessly looking for itself in superficial gratification of the senses. It is like gold-painted rocks being taken for real treasure; the rocks have no value and they keep soul hypnotized by their glitter and weighed down in the

Physical Plane. If a soul is mesmerized by its own reflection when it looks into the living waters of Spirit, it will not see the Face of God; and if it cannot see beyond its own ego, it will not be aware of God's plan for its life. God made soul in Its own Image and that Image is not found in a looking glass; it is a quality that has no reflection and cannot be admired and acknowledged, nor can it be flattered or bribed. For **love** is all that God sees in soul and all that will bring soul back into Its Heart. To merge consciously with the universal plans and become God-Absorbed, the participants of the Light and Sound must surrender all attachment to vanity of self and become as one who simply stands outside the influence of the mind and allows the gentle voice of Spirit to guide their actions day-by-day. It is only in releasing the little self in the looking glass that soul will see its true and divine nature in the clear, eternal waters that spring from the Heavenly Worlds of God.

The Light and Sound - unique in character and different in quality in this new Millennium

The new millennium brings with it a much higher rate of magnetic vibratory resonance than has ever before been manifested on Earth; it has expanded old vortices of energy and opened new ones that are capable of absorbing and channeling a stronger and more refined current of Light and Sound. This new current brings with it the ability to reintroduce the Miracles that were once so common on Earth. The heavy particles of atoms that make up the Physical Plane are moving at a more rapid rate of vibration and are more responsive to the focused application of thought driven by desire. One who is skilled in the art of manifestation will find a more malleable and receptive environment in which to perform their works.

Another aspect of the different quality of Light and Sound is an increase in telepathic communication. The purified atmosphere will make thought transference more agile from mind-to-mind and will increase the level of purity and understanding from heart-to-heart. This higher form of communication between souls will follow in direct alignment with the plans and mission of the Living Master, who is working on opening the hearts of the participants of the Light and Sound to receive more love and teach them the heart-to-heart transmission of expression that bypasses the mind and ego. In this environment of a new quality of Light and Sound, the quest for the development of the selfless heart will have the greatest chance for success as souls become more attuned to the finer elements of the spiritual currents that are flowing through their world and consciousness directly from the Godhead.

The development of higher soul creativity, thought, love and action to partner ourselves with the Consciousness of Sugmad, the Grand Council, and the Sehaji Hierarchies

"Love in Action" is the highest form of service to humanity and the highest level of communication with the Spiritual Hierarchies while inhabiting a human shell. Do all in the name of Love. Ask for nothing in return but to give for the sake of giving. Follow the example of Mother Theresa, who gave of herself 100% in all that she did to alleviate the suffering and poverty of those around her. She gave no thought to how she was perceived or acknowledged and sought only to exemplify the glory of the Lord that she so dearly loved. She acted with humility and grace and infinite patience and faith; for often times faith was her only lantern in the darkness. This does not mean that one must give their entire life to serving humanity in the way of this modern day saint, or that they must serve a spiritual Master like Jesus or even God Itself; any service done with love for its own sake is a force that stands on its own merit and is recognized by the Spiritual Hierarchies as an act of selflessness. The development of the selfless heart through acts of love toward others will stimulate higher soul creativity as each action grows from the dynamic of the previous one and new ways of living and giving are presented to the consciousness of soul.

Here follows a contemplative technique that will merge the participant consciously with Best-Laid Plans:

As given by Master Milarepa:

1. Imagine you are standing on a precipice gazing into a vast blue sky filled with stars. From out of the stars comes a bright sailing ship that flies through the air on invisible wings. It stops in front of you and you step onboard. The captain at the helm awaits you and can be any Spiritual Master of your choice.

2. And now you sail through the Inner realms until you see a Golden Temple of Wisdom in the far distance. As you approach it the Master of the temple comes out to greet you. This temple is Askleposis on the High Astral Plane and its Guardian is Gopal Das; this is where a section of the Best-Laid Plans of the Universe is stored and maintained. It is the section that is designated for the physical worlds.

3. Gopal takes your hand and leads you to the entrance of the building. As you step across the threshold, say this mantra three times: **"OLAY-VA-TU-MANA-TE."**

4. There is a holy enclave that holds a gold-crested book containing the Sacred Plans which can be viewed as a hologram. The book is on a table in front of an altar with two burning white candles on either side. There is a place to kneel in front of the book. Rest on your knees and simply ask to know the Plan for your life and how it can merge you with the plan for All Life. Ask to know your role in these holy plans of Sugmad. Stay in contemplation for as long as it feels right or until you have an answer. Many blessings are given you this day.

Here follows a contemplative technique that expands the participant into a feeling of Oneness with the Grand Council Heart Consciousness:

As given by Master Milarepa:

1. Imagine yourself lying on a grassy knoll on a warm, sunny day. You are gazing at the peaceful blue sky and

from the far horizon there comes an Eagle flying into your range of vision. Watch it fly overhead as it casts a golden aura over the lands with its tremendous and powerful wings.

2. Merge your consciousness with this graceful creature that represents the spiritual heart of the Grand Council. Simply watch it fly and feel yourself soaring with it above the clouds. At the same time, say this mantra aloud three times: **"SIVA-TU-ONA-HU-LE."**

3. Watch the Eagle and become one with its majestic journey across the horizon. Ask for a member of the Grand Council to speak to your heart about what you most need to know in this moment of time.

4. Stay in contemplation until the Eagle leaves the sky and you have a message imprinted upon your heart. Blessed Be.

~ ♥ ~

Paramitas, the Gathering of Many Rivers

~ Chapter Ten ~

Agam Des
and
Other Spiritual Cities

~ ♥ ~

The knowledge stored within the walls of Agam Des can change the course and destinies of entire worlds and planetary systems. This knowledge can only be gained by those who come in the name of truth and whose hearts have been thoroughly cleansed of all self-interests. This is a game only the strong in Spirit can play and the winning must be for the enrichment of all souls and life on all planes of reality.

~ ♥ ~

The spiritual city of Agam Des

Master Gopal Das:

Agam Des means "the inaccessible world" and it cannot be reached by ordinary means. It is a city within a city that harbors a secret passageway into the Eternal Truths of the Universe. Agam Des is the first great spiritual city of the Lower Worlds and is part of the supra-physical plane nestled within the Hindu Kush Mountains of Tibet. It can only be visited in the Soul Body by invitation and in the company of a Master of high spiritual merit. It was first constructed during the Antediluvian period which preceded the Great Flood of Noah as told of in Genesis of the Christian Bible. In that period of the Earth's history, people lived to be hundreds of years old and the lands were dominated by giants known as "Gibborim," the Hebrew word for "mighty." There was also the "Nephilim" race of peoples who were the offspring of divine-human relations and they are known in the spiritual hierarchy as the Olden Ones.

During the Antediluvian period of time, Agam Des was known as Mor Trelet – "the outer door to the Inner Kingdom". This city was the portico, the place of entrance, where the Olden Ones would meet for an initial summit to gather their forces of wisdom and carry it into the inner city, which became known as Agam Des for its inaccessibility to the outside world of men. Agam Des holds the secrets and mysteries of the ways of God; the Beings who inhabit this city are in charge of the cosmic forces that control the karmic destiny of mankind and of all life on Earth.

The spiritual leader of this great city is Yaubl Sacabi, a Master of great merit who is known to have been one of the original Olden Ones from the Antediluvian period. He is the one who chose the location for Agam Des deep within the mountains of Tibet where no human eyes can ever see its holy walls, nor human feet ever tread its sacred grounds. Only those souls with open hearts, pure and free of self-will can be allowed to enter this holy city in their Soul Bodies under the escort of an approved spiritual Master. Once inside, they will be taken to the Great Hall where the records of the mysteries of this world are kept and guarded by Master Lai Tsi. This is where they can study and reflect upon the wisdom and knowledge that this great city has harbored for eons.

The spiritual mission of Agam Des

Agam Des provides the doorway between the physical and non-physical worlds, and is a place of study for those who wish to understand the karmic destiny of Earth and humanity. It is also the place where history can be "manufactured" and processed to coincide with the Best-Laid Plans of this universe. At the time of its construction, the Earth was covered by a mist of micro-magnetic molecules of energy that moved in a random fashion; this energy carried the memories or "engrams" of all that had ever transpired on the planet. At Agam Des, this energy was harnessed and focused into a current that could carry the magnetic resonance of Earth's history and channel it into a predetermined destiny. In other words, karmic life and destiny are processed at Agam Des into past, present and future segments or "events" that can be experimented with and manipulated as necessary to stay in alignment with Best-Laid Plans. When the course of events on the Physical Plane begins to stray too far off center, it is given a transfusion of new energy and a new direction by the Master Planners at Agam Des who work with the cosmic forces that shape history and human destiny for the development of progress and the maintenance balance in the Lower Worlds. Agam Des reached full operation when the crucifixion of Jesus initiated Christianity's beginning.

Jesus will explain this release of energy further:

Jesus:

My crucifixion unleashed cosmic forces of nature that had been dormant for many centuries. I came into the world to re-awaken those forces which lay sleeping within the hearts of men; for it is humanity itself that has control over the energy that shapes and determines the manifestation of destiny. My job was to awaken the human heart to its true nature as a power circuit of love that moves mountains and builds civilizations, but more than that, the human heart has the power to create, control and manipulate the direction of world history in the making. The role of Christianity was to have been the catalyst for unlocking the secrets of the power of love within the heart of mankind, and to use it for the betterment of human and world conditions. This is what I had come to do and could have done more if my Life Contract had allowed me more latitude.

The spiritual path I created has been used as a power tool by the greedy and unscrupulous in certain historical epochs to further their own causes and leave destruction in their wake. It has been used to torment rather than comfort, and to keep souls in bondage rather than awaken them to the glory of the power within their own hearts and all it can do to achieve miracles in this world. The saints, prophets and holy people of Christianity have done everything they could to keep the vibrancy of love intact. It is the memories of their sacrifices and the love they have left that is keeping Christianity alive. My consolation is also in knowing that in Agam Des, my dreams for mankind are being realized in ways that surpass what I could have done on my own. And for that, I am eternally grateful.

The primary teachers of Agam Des

The primary teachers at Agam Des are the spiritual masters Lai Tsi, Gopal Das, Fubbi Quantz and Yaubl Sacabi, who is the guardian of the city. They are often joined by luminaries like Albert Einstein, Socrates, Plato; and scientists, philosophers and mathematicians from other galaxies. There are also teachers there whose names must remain secret because they currently walk among you.

Their fields of expertise range from science, astronomy, philosophy, physics and mathematics to metaphysics, time travel, prophecy, manifestation; and how to work with energy transference and transfusion, magnetic resonances, and how to harness and utilize cosmic forces.

Their duties entail facilitating talks and workshops on the above topics, which include preparing demonstrations and holographic "slide shows; one-on-one tutoring with gifted students; conducting guided tours for visiting dignitaries; performing scans on prospective visitors, as those who are impure in heart and full of ambition are simply not allowed into this city even for a glimpse; and working with the Lords of Karma to see that all knowledge shared in Agam Des is properly absorbed and used in a balanced manner.

Visitors from other galaxies

Visitors from other galaxies know that Agam Des is the storehouse for the secrets of this and all universes in the cosmos. It is a "one-stop shopping place" for knowledge and wisdom on any subject of spiritual importance and covers all the sciences and metaphysics of all the worlds and galaxies in creation. However, its doctrines are highly secret and much of what is contained there cannot be found anywhere else in existence; thus, it is highly coveted information and gives great power to the holder. The knowledge stored within the walls of Agam Des can change the course and destinies of entire worlds and planetary systems. This knowledge can only be gained by those who come in the name of truth and whose hearts have been thoroughly cleansed of all self-interests. This is a game only the strong in Spirit can play and the winning must be for the enrichment of all souls and life on all planes of reality.

The spiritual role of Agam Des compared to Ekere Tere

Master Gopal Das:

Agam Des is like the mast at the head of a sailing ship; it supports the sails, booms, rigging and signals and is what drives the vessel forward and gives it direction. Places like Ekere Tere would not be possible without the existence of Agam Des; it is the "forefather" of all spiritual cities in the worlds below the first Great Divide. While Ekere Tere has become the main vortex of spiritual education and learning, Agam Des maintains its position as "keeper of the spiritual flame" for all hidden knowledge of the ancient truths of this universe.

Master Treylor:

It is true that Agam Des is the masthead of the ship and that it holds great spiritual treasure, as yet unknown by mankind. The difference between the two spiritual cities is that the knowledge given at Ekere Tere is open to all qualified God seekers for their study and edification. The doors of Agam Des are not open or even visible to the general stream of consciousness. Ekere Tere was designed and located for the purpose of rebalancing the lost heart of Africa and restoring it to full capacity of operation. The vortex of energy at Ekere Tere is meant to spiritually cleanse the continent of Africa of the black magic that has plagued it for many centuries and return it to its former role of being the unifying force on Earth for love, freedom, truth and joy to come together.

Master Tremulen:

Agam Des is a place of research and development of plans and ideas that will create a greater expansion of life and opportunity for all souls in the universe. It is something like the special effects part of a movie production; it is the "light and magic" that gives the movie its depth and fascination; it moves it from the realm of the ordinary into the extraordinary, where all things are possible. That is my description of this great spiritual city: "The place where all things are made possible."

Master training in Agam Des

Agam Des offers a well-rounded training program on many subjects as previously discussed. There is no other spiritual city or wisdom temple on any plane of the universe with a range of knowledge as vast and varied as that found at Agam Des. This is also the place where the last shreds of dross in the soul consciousness can be dissolved and where a new magnetic signature can be given. Every Living Master leaves behind a part of their being that cannot be taken beyond their last level of Initiation. To become the Living Master, the old self must be eradicated and a new vibratory resonance must be set in place so that soul will be able to carry the mantle of the Rod of Power. This transformation of consciousness can be conducted in the laboratories at Agam Des under the supervision of the Olden Ones who have been performing this procedure for millions of years.

Remember that Agam Des is a "processing plant" of sorts; it can reconfigure world and planetary destinies and systems; and it can redesign the soul consciousness of an individual who is slated for an important role of spiritual leadership. New magnetic signatures are not given lightly and it requires the approval of the current Living Master who works in alignment with the Silent Nine, the Grand Council, and the Lords of Karma. Once that approval is given, the Olden Ones begin their work and a new Living Master steps forth at Agam Des.

The female Sehaji in Agam Des

The female Sehaji Masters (FSM's) - were each teamed with one of the Olden Ones who would serve as a mentor to their growth and development at Agam Des. This is often the case with spiritual masters who enter into training in this holy city; and it is especially so for the females who embark on a course of study that they be teamed with a Master of Old with male energy to balance and reinforce the feminine energy to withstand the high vibrational content of the knowledge at Agam Des, which is masculine in force and structure. Once this partnership is established between the female Sehaji Master and her male mentor, the FSM chooses a course of study that aligns with her specific skills and mission. For instance, if she is to serve on a planet in a far-distant galaxy, she is given access to that planet's genetic life code and karmic history, as well as its science and technology. Agam Des is the place where most Masters of the Sehaji have received their training and briefings. The FSM's training differs from their male counterparts in that they must undergo a transformation of consciousness that will accept the dominant male energy of the knowledge, wisdom and mysteries contained with Agam Des. When they complete this training, they are equipped to handle whatever storms they may encounter in the worlds they will visit and serve out their missions. The Male Sehaji go through the same processing of consciousness with their female aspect.

Brahm chose Agam Des as a primary meeting place with Catholic, Hindi, African and Eastern Saints, sages and teachers

Agam Des holds the key to universal brotherhood because of its resources to shape human destiny; it can mold and define karmic and historical aspects of life on Earth. When Brahm sees the need for divine intervention in the progress of mankind, He invites the Saints, Sages and Teachers of the major world religions to come to Agam Des and discuss where they are in terms of the progress of their spiritual paths and teachings, and what needs to be done to bring those paths into greater alignment with Best-Laid Plans. Each Master Teacher brings their own unique perspective and experience into the mix so a course of action can be determined that will open their teachings to receive the proper adjustment of calibrations necessary to bring them into a higher frequency of Light and Sound vibration that can be carried back to Earth and distributed to their participants and followers. This is one of the ways that Brahm likes to maintain balance in the Lower Worlds – by utilizing and distributing the unique energetic frequencies available at Agam Des to mold and shape the evolvement of

His worlds. He requires the cooperation of the Spiritual Leaders of mankind to synchronize their energies with the flow of His will and design. Some of these plans are so secret that they can only be maintained in a city like Agam Des with nearly inaccessible entry except by invitation; and so the great Brahm chooses this highly guarded spiritual city as the primary meeting place with the Saints, Sages and Teachers from around the globe to discuss world destiny and evolution.

Buddha's teachings in Agam Des

Buddha is a wise and joyful soul who looks at the world as his "playground". He has always sought the more joyous aspects of living and likes the idea of playing with the mysteries of life; he likes to take it to the limit of what he can do with shaping the historical and karmic content of reality and spends endless hours in the laboratories of Agam Des creating worlds of his design and desire. Some of these worlds have remained prototypes and have not been given life, while others have taken form and substance and exist alongside this world as "parallel realities." Buddha is one of those Masters who governs Fate and Choice in the destiny of mankind. He believes that each soul is their own God and creates from within them the world they choose to inhabit. He is a great believer in self-governance and the quest for personal and spiritual happiness. He likes the vast opportunities at Agam Des for transforming and manipulating karma and destiny, and it is from this platform of unlimited freedom that the great Buddha chooses to speak to his disciples about creating love, joy, abundance and personal freedom in their lives; and about finding the "Buddha" within.

Revelations and the Seer of Patmos

The Book of Revelations in the Christian Bible is about the meaning of history in God's plan for the world; it encompasses the destiny of mankind and its karmic ramifications. The Olden Ones of Agam Des decided it was time to shake the earth world from its lethargy and they chose the Apostle John as their messenger of truth for those times. John had spiritual abilities only Christ knew of; for instance, he knew the secret of how to make invisible that which is apparent only to the physical eyes. He would be the one to harness the power of Revelation contained in the energetic frequencies at Agam Des and funnel them into the structure of the written word. John went to the Seer of Patmos for the unveiling of Revelations; the Seer's identity has long been held a secret. Much of what is contained in Revelations came to be when the **Seven Seals** of the Book of Secrets was broken by Christ Jesus through the power of His own Knowledge and Resurrection; and God's Word and Best-Laid Plans were brought forth into the Lower Worlds. The training of John to work with the forces of Revelation at Agam Des was overseen mainly by Yaubl Sacabi and Gopal Das.

Entrance into Agam Des

Entry is determined by a scanning process conducted by one of the Resident Masters. The scan not only reveals dross or blockages in the magnetic resonance of the Inner bodies of that soul, but has the capacity to "remove" them under certain circumstances and then "replace" them as the individual is ready to take their leave. In other words, **no one** is allowed entry into Agam Des without a "clean slate" of consciousness. The process of removal and replacement of negative energy is used for visitors and temporary residents who have not yet reached Mastership status, and whose purpose for entry is to study under an apprenticeship with one of the Masters or begin training with them, or participate in one of the many "roundtable" discussions that are always in progress at Agam Des. All others who enter the city must be of the 9th Initiation and above, and must have a serious purpose for their visit that meets with the approval of the main Guardian, Yaubl Sacabi. As yet, there are no "guided tours" available for those who are merely curious to see inside Agam Des. For those souls who want a glimpse, they can work with their Spiritual Teachers or the Living Master who can give them the proper exercise to that effect. Agam Des will never be an amusement park and is only for the most serious of ventures.

Here follows a spiritual exercise that will allow the God seeker a glimpse or a chance to walk the streets of Agam Des

As given by Master Milarepa:

1. Imagine you are on a tiger hunt. You are walking through a jungle of lush green plants and colorful flowers. You are seeking the great Bengal Tiger who wears a crown of rubies and emeralds. There are

many tigers roaming the jungle, but only one who wears the crown. Seek him out; he will come to you when you say this mantra three times: "**DOMINAY-PLATU-AGAM-DES.**"

2. Now he appears and you can approach this majestic beast without fear. He bows and allows you to climb upon his back. You ride with him through the maze of the jungle that gets deeper and more difficult to navigate. At times you can barely see through the tangle of wild undergrowth, trees and foliage. But soon there comes a clearing and a white stone door becomes visible through a soft, golden mist. Here the tiger leaves you. Approach the door and say this mantra three times: "**MANATAY-SI-PLATU-AGAM-DES.**"

3. Now the door begins to open very slowly, so slowly that you must strain to see what lies beyond. **Now sing HU five times and then sing Dan Rin five times.** Keep looking. If your heart is open and filled with love, you may be allowed to catch a glimpse or even walk the streets of this magnificent and forbidden city. Stay in this contemplation for at least fifteen minutes. If nothing comes, try again for the next six days. May you be blessed by all that is Holy.

~♥~

Paramitas, the Gathering of Many Rivers

Chapter Eleven

Shamballa, Home of the White Brotherhood

~♥~

The role of Shamballa is to provide a fortress for peace; giving it the power of a thousand thunders to move and shake the Earth from its self-destructive stupor. We are Lions who lead the Shepherds of Peace to gather their flocks to safety once more.

~♥~

Shamballa, chosen as the "Home of the White Brotherhood"

As given by Sri Yukteswar, guru of Yogananda, and author of *The Holy Science*:

Shamballa, the City of Peace and Harmony, was designed to connect Eastern and Western religious philosophies and establish a common ground of spiritual understanding and unity. It is the place where the Great White Brotherhood has its meeting ground and is the foundation for the propagation of peace to unify all parts of the world. My great interest in this spiritual city is the ability to connect with like hearts and minds to work to erase the divisions of understanding among souls who are returning home to God. My goal with Yogananda and the Brotherhood is to promote religious unity and peace among men. That was Yogananda's great purpose in the West - to open the gates of spiritual understanding with the East and bring the Eastern religious philosophy into Western culture in a way that would be easy to digest. He fulfilled his mission with flying colors and I am supremely proud of his accomplishments. I take no credit for them; he always had the wings to fly – I simply pointed him in the right direction. Our work here at Shamballa is multi-faceted and includes close interaction with the White Brotherhood, as we are both members of this Great Spiritual Order and have the honor to speak as one voice on their behalf.

The role of the White Brotherhood at Shamballa

Sri Yukteswar and Dan Rin:

We are the Keepers of the Flame of Peace among men and women on Earth. We work with the Archangel Hierarchies and move the tides of whole nations toward finding peaceful resolutions to their stormy seas of warfare and strife. We also work one-on-one with individual leaders – political and spiritual – and invite them to Shamballa for discussions. Most leaders accept our invitations with alacrity and are willing to work with us, but some are stubborn and refuse to obey the summons. Leaders such as Adolph Hitler and Idi Amin were two such individuals who chose to take the path of self-destruction and annihilation of all that is good and holy in order to perpetuate their delusions of grandeur and lust for power and control. The power mongers of the world are not interested in the goals we set at Shamballa, but ultimately cannot escape them. Today Hitler sits up to his neck in the human decay of the lives he destroyed and will not be heard from again for a very long time. This is his own doing as the spiritual laws are absolute and demand restitution for wrongs committed against the Holy Spirit.

The builders of Shamballa

Sri Yukteswar and Dan Rin:

Shamballa was built by the great races that once inhabited the lost continents of Atlantis and Lemuria. It was laid stone-by-stone by the power of crystal energy and never a human hand was put to the task. The resonance of the energy it took to build the city has a residual effect on the life span of its inhabitants; the buildings emanate the energy of the crystals that were used in its construction. It was built as a Fortress of Peace that could be easily accessed by all worthy seekers of God. Shamballa sits in a vortex of the High Astral Plane between India and Tibet because that is where the greatest force of spiritual wisdom, focus and power is concentrated. Most of the Avatars of peace, love and brotherhood get their training here. The crusades such as the Peace Movement of the 1960's, Women's Rights, Civil Rights, the Geneva Convention, etc., all started here.

The city of Shamballa is stepping forward

This is the time when the Lion must take back control of the Jungle; it has been left in the hands of chimpanzees for too long, and so strength and leadership must once again take hold in the worlds of man. I have watched the wars of the 20th century turn the soil of Eastern Europe, Africa and the Middle East red with the blood of human death and destruction. The wheels of war are turning mercilessly and must be stopped before there will be no turning back to peace and prosperity for the men and women on Earth. The role of Shamballa is to provide a fortress for peace, giving it the power of a thousand thunders to move and shake the Earth from its self-destructive stupor. We are Lions who lead the Shepherds of Peace to gather their flocks to safety once more. You can see our influence in the current political race in the United States; for the first time in history a man of the black race and a woman are running for the office of President of that country. We are shaking and waking up the consciousness of mankind and we have chosen the strongest country on Earth with which to begin this great transformation. We are keeping the waters calm for the political race to come to its pre-destined conclusion, and hearts that would have remained closed and even protested in violence are now ready to receive a black man as president. This is progress! And there will be more in store for the great country of America and the rest of the world as the plans of the White Brotherhood continue to unfold.

What inspired Sri Yukteswar to reach the upper rungs of the God Worlds and to serve humanity

Sri Yukteswar:

I was inspired from childhood when I saw the seeming inequality and suffering of those who begged on the streets of Calcutta. To me, they were lacking more than food or money; they had a deep unquenchable need and thirst for God. I knew from that early age that I must do something to relieve that need for God in hungry souls. I met my guru, Lahiri Mahasaya, in the dream state at age 18. I often walked with him along the reflection of the Ganges River on the Astral Plane. He spoke to me in volumes of riddles and equations that I would have to solve in my waking life. Each night for 20 years he gave me a question to ponder and resolve until I had reached a level of understanding where I could easily comprehend the truth behind every illusion of Maya in my daily life and in the lives of those who sought my counsel. All feeling and perception of lack in man is an illusion. All suffering is not based on truth; it is only man's longing for God in all things outside of himself that causes pain. God is within the heart and soul of man and no one is "rich or poor" in God's Kingdom – all are endowed with the treasures of Divine Mercy, Love and Abundance. There are no beggars on the streets of heaven. I wanted to bring that heaven to Earth and teach the suffering ones to claim their divine heritage as sons and daughters of the One God.

My goal has always been to seek the underlying unity in all religious teachings and to fill the hearts of men with spiritual wisdom that encompass the truth within all worthy religions and erase the lines of division, discord and misunderstanding. I teach my students to seek the common ground of the many pathways to God and build a unifying link through deep communion with divine love, tolerance and compassion. It was my dream to unite Eastern spiritual wisdom with Western technology and science as a way to alleviate human suffering on the spiritual, psychological and material levels, and to promote Inner growth toward Self-Realization. That dream came true when my disciple, Yogananda, came to the West and built his three fortresses of spiritual understanding where people of all cultural backgrounds could study and learn the wisdom of the ages that has no geographical or socio-political boundaries.

The virtues Sri Yukteswar is looking for in his students

Those who wish to study with me are chosen by virtue of their intense and selfless desire to serve God in all ways.

They must demonstrate right thinking and discernment; obey the Law of Silence by not indulging in idle chatter or gossip; show humility and grace under all conditions; be patient and self-sacrificing in putting the needs of others ahead of their own (as in working for the highest good of all concerned) wherever possible. They must show strength and independence of character while staying balanced and willing to obey the instruction of their spiritual Teachers. Good humor is always a plus – one should not get carried away with his own self-importance or get bogged down in methodology, dogma or rhetoric. The heart stays open when the face is smiling with joy for the love of service to God. Put God first above all things and seek Him out in the smallest flower or blade of grass. Let the love for God shine like a lantern from your being and light the way for others to follow in your holy footsteps. You have my blessings and grace.

The duties of Sri Yukteswar in Shamballa

I teach the higher laws of science, religion and metaphysics to those students who wish to open the gates of spiritual knowledge that can be assessed and accepted by the skeptical Western mind. The West leads the consciousness of the world and its scientists hold the key to probing outside the boundaries of the visible, tangible world into the invisible and intangible cosmic realities. I teach my students to raise thought-provoking questions and theories that will bridge the gap between science and metaphysics. I want the logical thinkers of the West to abandon their immutable laws and embrace the cosmic possibilities of soul beyond the body, life beyond death, spirit beyond nature. Mathematical science was developed by man to make sense of the physical world of time and space through the systematic arrangement of facts and general laws. This is the grounding point for all scientific research and thought processes, and it is from this point that man is compelled to seek the deeper meaning behind that which has no scientific explanation. My students are taught how to stimulate the desire in others to understand spiritual phenomena and seek the truth behind its mysteries. There will come a day when miracles will be commonplace and there will be no more division between scientific knowledge and spiritual wisdom. These will blend into a common truth so that man is no longer ignorant of realities that exist beyond the five physical senses. My work is to unify science with spirituality and to show modern man that his physical world has a spiritual counterpart, and that his origin, being and destiny is that of pure spirit and oneness with God.

Entry into the White Brotherhood

Master Tremulen:

There must be first and foremost a great desire to serve mankind as protectors, guardians, wayshowers and teachers. This requires courage, trust, perseverance, wisdom and the ability to lead others. Experience in teamwork as part of a religious or spiritual order is a prerequisite to joining the White Brotherhood. This is a group dynamic - there is no hierarchy in this holy order - all are parts of the whole and equally necessary for the successful completion of its goals and missions. Thus, all egos are left at the door, as only those of great humility and fair-mindedness are allowed entrance. The White

Brotherhood has no set number of members and it changes in size according to need. There are members from all points of the universe and from other galaxies and star systems; they can be male or female, but are mostly of the male energy. Not all members are human, and some come from the future. Some souls have been in the White Brotherhood for many centuries and some are newly arrived and must be initiated into its Ways and Creed to serve and protect. They are given an Oath by one of the Templar Knights and touched on each shoulder by the Sword of Righteousness. Thus knighted, a soul becomes one with the mission of the White Brotherhood and takes their place as a Warrior and Light Giver for the cause of universal peace, balance, unity, salvation and protection. It is important to understand The White Brotherhood is different from the White Robe Hierarchy; our function is the regulation of this physical universe's balance. The White Robe functions on both rungs of the universes of Sugmad.

The White Brotherhood and their art of healing

Jesus used "Talfiq" - he could heal with the eyes, hands and voice, and could also project out of the body to heal the negative engrams at the point of the resonating origin of the illness on the Inner. The latter was accompanied by the use of sacred mantras that he learned from Archangel Gabriel and other mentors.

Jesus:

In addition to the above, I worked with the heart energy of the recipients in an open-and-closing sequence of energetic transfusion from my own heart to theirs. It is not easy to explain, but the flow of healing energy had to be regulated very carefully and not given at once, but in increments that were modulated for that particular individual's rate of absorption. Once I saw with my Inner eyes that they had reached their capacity to absorb the healing I was sending them, I ended the process; so not all healings were "complete" in that the malady could return again at a later time, but for those recipients who could absorb the full flow of healing resonance that was required, the illnesses were healed completely and forever.

Sri Yukteswar:

I was instructed by my guru, Lahiri Mahasaya and *paramguru,* Babaji (the guru of my guru) on how to heal the various inconsistencies within the physical and subtle bodies of man. I used an open-and-closing method similar to that of the Christ as I worked with the chakras of those who came to me for healing. I prefer the chakra method of healing, because much of what ails man is karmic energy trapped within the vortices of the body. You can see this energy as a dark mass upon the auric field that gathers in the chakras. I would stand close to the ones seeking release from suffering and raise the vibration of their consciousness to a level where they as soul could heal themselves. At other times I would lay my hands on the afflicted area; it depended on the individual needs of the person. Many times I performed remote healing by transmitting a high energetic frequency that the subtle bodies of the person could receive and impart to the physical body and loosen the hold of the karmic pattern causing the illness. All spiritual healing is done through the use of rates and frequencies of energetic transmission to key places within the auric fields of the individual. It is all a matter of adjusting the vibrations of the life forces and vortices within the invisible bodies of man. Healing has nothing to do with "flesh and blood" – that is an effect and not a cause. Man is made up of millions of invisible atoms of moving energy that must be regulated by proper thought, conduct, diet and exercise. When any of these are out of alignment, illness sets in and it is simply a matter of re-aligning the delicate atomic structure and balance of the body to affect healing.

I use an ancient Vedic method that was taught to me by Babaji in which I work with the atoms of the soul body of the recipient and restructure them to be able to absorb more light. Illness causes density and stagnation of the movement of the atoms, and so I open that energy through the chakras and "guide it" to the areas in need of healing. As this energy is moving through the body, I make adjustments to the magnetic resonance surrounding that energy by sound techniques such as powerful mantras. Sound is the moving force of all energy within the bodies of man; the proper use of sound opens the space to receive more light and a higher resonance takes place which releases illness of physical and spiritual origins. The malady is then neutralized and shifted to another location outside of that person's body.

The concept of God's Love

The love for God is very simple in theory but not so simple in action - it is giving of oneself without thought of return. To truly give is a concept that most people do not fully understand. They think it is enough to share a material possession, to share food, time or company, but true giving goes beyond the material plane of cause and effect; it is a function of the higher self which resides in the God planes where mind has no jurisdiction and all is done from the soul consciousness rather than the personality. So if I were to give you an apple when you are hungry, have I truly given you something? Or have I simply fulfilled a temporary need? There is a significant difference between filling a need and "giving." If I have given the apple with a blessing, I have given food to the **soul** of the person as well as their body. Therein lies the difference - what is attached or not attached to the act of giving - is it a conscious act of love or is it the desire to feel good about yourself?

So that is one aspect of the Love for God - the act of giving with love from the soul consciousness without thought of the self. The other part of the equation is the act of "receiving" the gift. This is a world of dual realities and each action must have a positive and equal reaction for the process to be complete. So, giving with love must also be received with love, so that God has attained full expression in the transaction. When you bless what you bestow on another, you are relating to their higher self and it is that higher aspect of the person that responds to your gesture of love whether they are aware of it or not. This creates a full circle of divine love for God and His creation, and opens a channel for more love to come into this world moment by moment.

Sri Yukteswar's *The Holy Science*

I was inspired by the great Avatar, Babaji, who approached me to write this book. I thought at first there were minds greater than mine who could do the work better justice, but found upon embarking on the project that it fell perfectly into line with my soul consciousness and understanding. It is not a book for the general public, because it does not address the physical mind of man, but rather his higher self and it is from that perspective that the book can best be absorbed and understood. It is an exercise in contemplative introspection, meaning that the contents are best absorbed when pondered from the state of meditation, a few lines at a time.

I am pleased with the reception of this book because it fulfilled the desire of my paramguru, Babaji, to address knowledge that had not been given light before then. It was meant as a stimulus to the consciousness of man to look deeper into the mysteries of life and of his place in the grand design as set by God. I also wanted to build the bridge between science and religion to show that there is no division between the physical and spiritual realities, that all is one and heading in the same direction. All science is the desire to uncover the truth of the mystery of life, which is God. And so there is really no difference between the goals of scientific research and the goals of the great world religions. My book is the bridge that connects these two powerful forces in the search for reunion of man with God, and I am happy if one person gained inspiration from its contents.

Future agenda of the White Brotherhood

Dan Rin and Archangel Gabriel:

The work of the White Brotherhood (WB) can be seen in the changing consciousness of American politics where they now have a woman and a black man running for the highest office in the land in present day 2008. This is the signature of brotherhood among men - to abandon all forms of prejudice and embrace the body of soul within man and woman. The WB has sanctioned this political race and works behind the scenes to encourage open-hearted communication between the candidates and their constituents. A wave of HU is constantly flowing through the efforts of this presidential race because this time in history is crucial for the survival of America and its position as a world superpower. The American economy has been crippled by the war waged in Iraq and an immediate turnaround must be established to literally save the country from economic ruin. The WB feels that a Democratic president can restore balance to the US, both economically and in its relationship with the rest of the world. The Illuminati and Skull & Cross Bones Societies of America's elite schools have not decided the full course of their political agenda until free will settles the dust in the present politics of American politics. They are conferring with their European counterparts as to how this will affect the future of the British pound, yen and euro dollar. The deciding factor will be America's unified consciousness and who stands behind the next five presidents. The latter's societies' agenda is as longstanding as the Pilgrims' landing on Plymouth Rock; their hand of influence is invisible yet strong, and not to be underestimated in economic and political latitude.

There is a rising threat to world peace brewing in China, where economic prosperity is catapulting that country into a position of strength and domination. The WB is attempting to bridle that growth because China is the potential birth place for the next world dictator. If prosperity ensues without a balanced competitor, nationalism will influence them to an attempt to conquer the world. China will need another prosperous nation with a strong military to balance their world position. China's prosperity will be unrivaled if the British pound and the euro go bankrupt. So this is an area of major concern to the WB that is working around the clock to monitor, guide and control this potentially explosive situation.

Another area of concern is the subjugation of women in the Middle East. The Arabic world is watching closely to see if a woman becomes president of the United States. This will have a significant impact on the rights and freedom of Arabic women because of the vibration that will begin to change the consciousness of how women are viewed around the world. This truly is the Century of the Woman and this has long been a labor of love by the White Brotherhood to restore the status of power and strength to the feminine energy and nature of womanhood.

The WB is also working to control and eradicate the plagues of disease and famine in the African nations. This is very close to the heart of the Living Master, whose mission is to free Africa from black magic and promote its renaissance. Africa is the heartbeat of the Earth and all energy flows from and to this maternal and nurturing vortex of the planet. The WB works closely with the Brown and Green Robes, who oversee the healing of the rich African soil and all that it produces so that there is a "green" foundation of fertility to uphold the body of mother Africa and cleanse her of poisons that have drained her strength for many centuries. The Renaissance of Africa is connected to the resurgence of power in women around the world. The Earth must regain its feminine energy to balance the overcharged male energy that has long dominated the Physical Plane. All these things work in unison and are overseen by the Masters of the White Brotherhood who have much on their table and much in store for the return of a peaceful co-existence of humanity on earth.

The universal mission of the White Brotherhood

The White Brotherhood is made up largely of those who have served as warriors, knights, soldiers and others of military skills whose role it has been to fight for the cause of justice and to protect the rights and sanctity of life on Earth. These are brave and courageous souls who have given up their lives for the sake of freedom and peace. They have long carried the sword of righteousness into battle and know how to balance injustice with the least amount of casualties to human life and destruction of land and property. What separates them from mercenaries or soldiers of fortune is the **vibration of divine service** they carry in their hearts. These are missions from the Godhead that are given with great responsibility and solemn trust. The Order of the Red Dragon and Gabriel counsel and at times direct the White Brotherhood because Sugmad wants this battle to be won between the forces of Light and

Darkness; Light must win at all costs. The WB knows how to get it done in the most effective and efficient ways possible and with spiritual power and resolution.

To the brethren of the White Brotherhood still in their physical shells

St. Francis of Assisi speaks:

In my short lifetime on Earth I found that the greatest force in the world is selfless love and doing all things in the name of Divine Service to God. See God in all faces and places on your journeys. Do not be fooled by those who would threaten or taunt you; they are meek as lambs under the cover of the wolf. If you shine the light of God ever before you, all darkness flees from your path and it is lit by the protection of His Grace and Mercy. Anger and hatred are nothing to fear for the one who sees only love in all things. True, there is great evil in the world, but it is of the temporal and unstable forces of duality that vanish when faced with the presence of the Eternal. So, bless each day with the light of God and do all in His Name. There is no greater shield, sword, ammunition or weaponry of any kind than the Word and Armor of your Father in Heaven. He will protect the faithful and lead them from the bowels of hell to the High Ground of Love, Compassion and Eternal Salvation.

Facing daily challenges

Archangel Gabriel:

One thing I have found helpful is to begin each day with a highly-charged spiritual mantra that brings in the clear light of soul and cleanses the chakras such as the Root Clearing technique as given by Agnotti that rids the Inner bodies of accumulated dross, and which can be found in the spiritual exercises of The Way of Truth. It is very hard to see clearly through a dirty window and so it is recommended that the God seeker begin by clearing their aura of trapped or stale energy. This allows the physical body to perform more efficiently and improves the thought processes, and the ability to transmit and receive instruction from the Masters of the Universal Mind. A God seeker whose mission it is to balance the Earth must be able to receive spiritual direction and guidance clearly and must himself be a clear channel for Divine Will and Purpose. Once a state of Inner balance and receptivity is achieved, it is easier to overcome daily challenges by understanding the nature of their origins and simply allowing them to play out in the arena of life as the God seeker "watches from a distance" – which means going through them with detachment and giving all to the flow of Spirit within the Light and Sound.

I would also recommend daily exercises that expand the heart's capacity to understand the nature of others. There are many such exercises in The Way of Truth and one can also make up their own by simply closing their eyes, breathing deeply and concentrating on the Third Eye between the eyebrows. Then sing a holy word such as HU or any word of spiritual merit that brings in a feeling of upliftment, and ask to understand the hearts of others. I find that the simpler the exercise, the greater is the affect as simplicity bypasses the mind's desire to analyze and control information. Eventually you will be able to see into another person's heart as they speak, and you will "hear" beyond the words and "know" what they are truly thinking and feeling. This is a vital aspect of working to balance the Earth, because it begins with the inhabitants – it begins with seeking the heart of love in all people and their experiences.

Herein follows a contemplative exercise will expand the individual's creativity of his or her spiritual mission

1. Imagine what looks like a huge Sundial lying in the middle of a field of green grass on a sunny day. As you approach the Dial, you see it is divided into sections of service to mankind, such as teacher, healer, speaker, etc. There are many roles to choose from.

2. Walk to the center of the Dial and say this mantra three times: **"SULE-MANNA-RE-TA"** (pronounced sulay mannah ray tah.")

3. Now see where the sun places your shadow; what field of service is it in? You may have to do this exercise several times for the right field to reveal itself. This will stimulate your creativity as the many forms of service

begin to reflect from your soul consciousness to your mind and appear on the Dial.

Herein follows a contemplative exercise to request entry into the divine city of Shamballa and gain training under one of its many spiritual teachers

1. Imagine you are a passenger waiting for a train to take you to Shamballa. You stand before golden railroad tracks that shimmer with a spiritual luminescence. From the far distance you hear the haunting sound of the train whistle like a mantra of peace and solitude. You see the train approaching – a magnificent silver vehicle with clear, shining windows. It stops in front of you and the door opens for you to enter.

2. Go inside and take a seat by a window. Now it begins to roll toward your destination and the only thing missing is the ticket for entrance. Call the Conductor forth who has your ticket in his possession. Say this mantra three times: **"VO-TE-LA-TU-SHAMBALLA."**

3. The Conductor appears before you and places the ticket for entry into Shamballa in your open hand. It is white with gold lettering and has your name in the center. That is enough to get you in.

4. Now the train stops at the gates to your divine destination. Walk to the gate and give the Guardian your holy ticket. That is all that is required for entrance into this great spiritual city. A Master will be waiting to

escort you and provide whatever training you need at this time. Go with peace and love in your heart!

Chapter Twelve

Nampak, an Angelic Waystation

~ ♥ ~

Love is the most powerful force in existence and it creates as well as destroys what is necessary to keep of all balance and harmony in God's Unlimited Creation.

~ ♥ ~

Nampak as an angelic waystation

Nampak is a spiritual or "angelic" waystation for those souls who have crossed over under traumatic circumstances. It is a small monastic community that gives comfort to those souls who experienced a traumatic death. The Angelic authorities assist in soul's transition into the upper regions of the Astral, Causal and Mental Planes. It is the realm where the greatest concentration of healing energy exists and not only serves to heal individual souls, but can affect entire regions and populations by the waves of vibration that are emitted like radio waves from a tower.

The importance of Nampak to present day Africa

Nampak is in a vortex over the Congo-Zaire region of Africa which is facing a political bloodbath between two major political factions. Enough attention of the Light and Sound coming from this vortex could bring peace and economic balance to this region. The contingent free will can be influenced by love to pressure these groups to go the peace table and sort out their differences.

The power of contemplation

Archangel Gabriel:

The projectory use of love has been a tool that Masters have used since the dawn of mankind to balance the course of human affairs. Without it, there would be total chaos of the apocalyptic kind where men would be reduced to savages fighting for survival. The use of this spiritual tool is done *en masse* by the Masters in charge of keeping law and order in the Universe and it is also done on an individual basis by God seekers of the Light and Sound who are trained in its use. A powerful mantra is used to stimulate the pineal gland behind the eyes and once it is vibrating at the optimal level, love is projected from the Third Eye directly to a focused destination. Those with clairvoyant vision can see the light projections that look similar to the beams of light that emanate from the headlamps of mine workers. These light beams have different colors, depending on the frequency and caliber of love, and range from the palest pink to the deepest rose. Once projected to their target, a wave of divine energy is released around that person, group, or area that brings in new components of Light and Sound that restructure the magnetic resonance in the environment, attracting new and better conditions.

Contemplative projectory of love has been used to win important battles in war that have a pivotal effect on the course of history. It has been used to clear an entire country from destructive Inner or Outer forces which would have destroyed its inhabitants and resources, and even to prevent world annihilation from the atom bomb and nuclear wars. Love is the most powerful force in existence and it creates as well as destroys what is necessary to keep of all balance and harmony in God's Unlimited Creation. Its projected use must be carefully monitored and performed only by those who are well trained in this procedure. For the soul who has yet to reach Mastership status, love can be given through the heart by various methods of spiritual exercises like those found in The Way of Truth. All good people can give love to one another in the ways closest to their own nature; a mere thought of love can change an entire environment for the better. Give love wisely to all in your day and do all in the name of the One God, the Sugmad; then only the highest results will prevail.

The African Masters Towart Managi and Arutu speak of their spiritual missions to assist their African brothers and sisters of the Light and Sound of God

Master Towart Managi and Master Arutu:

Our mission is to lift the veil of darkness and despair from the hearts of the African people by going among them into the remotest villages and giving hope where there is desperation, sustenance where there is famine, and relief where there is plague and pestilence. We have recruited invisible Light Workers who are restructuring the environment through the use of projected love as described earlier. We work alongside the Lords of Karma to see exactly where and with which souls we can make changes. We do a lot of work with life contracts to help individual souls in Africa transform their karma within the structure of Best-Laid Plans. There are many loopholes we can manipulate and adjust to relieve suffering where it is no longer necessary for spiritual growth. We also work with "karmic loops" that keep our brothers and sisters in Africa in endless cycles of despair and poverty so that they may be released to find greater opportunities for a better life. We are of the "hands on" School of Mastery and believe in working side-by-side with those who need our help. We want to see from their perspective what is going on in their lives so that we can make the best choices possible to serve their interests and uplift their life conditions. We walk invisibly among the African people giving hope and blessings to all in our path. We have also on occasion taken on human forms and held the hands of the dying as they crossed over into the worlds of Spirit. We have comforted the old, and sick and lame, and have held little children with love and bestowed many blessings of protection. The course of a single life can be forever transformed by our presence. We find it takes but a small seed of love given from a selfless heart to create a garden of hope, change and salvation. So we are the Seed Planters who help the African people harvest love from the soil of their lives and are their saving grace in every day living.

Always remember that each day has a sunset and each sunset has a new day to follow. Do all that you can within each day and then allow yourself to rest with the setting of the sun. There is no need to carry your burdens into the night. Sleep under the protection of the stars and know there is a new dawn that will rise along with you and light your way all through the day until it is time to rest again. Let nothing deter you from finding the heart of peace in your daily activities. This can be accomplished by doing all in the name of God, in the name of Love for the Divine One who tenderly cares for you at all times, whether you are aware of the gentle Presence or not. Dear Brothers and Sisters of Africa, you are not forgotten children! Your Father of the Light and Sound watches over you and has sent his beloved emissary, Dan Rin, to be your champion and fight for your spiritual freedom and your life's salvation. Be comforted and of good cheer, for this life is but a temporal dream. Play your part with courage and faith and you will be led to the Kingdom of the Promised

Land where a place is waiting for you in the heart of Love, Mercy and Eternal Peace.

For healers being trained at Nampak

Many psychic healers damage their emotional bodies by not clearing themselves and their physical environment. The first rule of thumb for all healing practitioners: do not perform acts of healing in your home, if it is at all possible. We know of some practitioners who have been very successful with home practices but there is always the possibility of entity-squatters invading the home, so spiritual clearing is vital. There is a residual negative energy that is released during the healing process and attaches itself to people and environments; it is very hard to dispose of, especially from the environment. So never do healing work in your home unless all areas of protection have been provided for; nor is it recommended to go to the client's home. It is best to work from a neutral place such as an office or even in the outdoors so that negative energy will more easily dissipate and not be attracted to the magnetic resonance of a person's home environment. Not every entity afflicting its victim will stand by dormant while their feeding ground is taken away. Some entities have the capacity to strike back at the healing practitioner with physical force.

It is important for all healing practitioners to establish a relationship with the Oversouls of the clients who come to them for relief. This Oversoul is often known as the person's guardian angel or can be their spiritual teacher. Without the cooperation of the Oversoul, no healing can take place. There is a simple protocol for speaking to the

Oversoul; one must show courtesy, love and respect for the relationship that the Oversoul has with its physical aspect. This can be as simple as saying, "I ask your permission to perform this healing." Then sing five HU's and wait for the Inner nudge to proceed; the healer will know it is all right by the feeling of lightness and love in the area of the solar plexus. If there is a feeling of heaviness, tightness or "dread" in that area, it is best to wait for another time to do the work.

It is good for healers to have knowledge of the invisible forces that awaken when they begin to move energetic reference points of energy. One way to have this understanding is for the practitioner to find out what Masters are working with them behind the scenes; for they can rest assured that there are invisible Beings working with them and through them. The Order of the Brown Robes wants their healing channels to be knowledgeable of the spiritual laws that govern their specific hierarchy and there are classes on the Inner planes where that knowledge can be attained. Nampak offers many such classes and it is a matter for the healer to say before going to sleep that they wish to attend a "Brown Robe Healing Seminar". They will then be led in the soul body to the class that is best for them at that point in their development.

Much of what goes on in the healing profession cannot be seen or witnessed by the physical eyes. There is intensive Inner training going on at all times and this is the only way that Sugmad will allow healing practices to prosper and succeed in the Lower Worlds. Otherwise there would be much mayhem done to the karmic fabric of individuals and to the Best-Laid Plans of the universe.

Herein follows a contemplative exercise that will enable those who have the purity of heart the means to work with Arutu and Towart Managi in this spiritual movement for Africa's Renaissance

1. Imagine you are on a small boat or canoe which is gliding silently along a peaceful river. There is a definite destination ahead and you can feel it pulling you along effortlessly; it fills you with increasing peace and joy the closer you get to it. The sounds of the waters are like a lullaby to the soul and you are serenely guided and protected on this journey. You have only to surrender, relax, and go with the flow of the river.

2. Now you come to a bridge that crosses over the river. Two Masters stand at the center of the bridge - Arutu and Towart Managi. They smile and raise their hands in greeting. As they do, your boat is guided to the riverbank and you get out and walk to the bridge. As you step onto it, say this mantra three times: "**SULU-TU-MANA-TU-ARA-TE.**"

3. Now you are free to approach the Masters and they embrace you warmly. **Ask what you can do to help them in the spiritual movement toward the great African Renaissance.** That is all that is required, dear Brothers and Sisters of the Light and Sound. May God bless you in all that you do in His Holy Name.

~❤~

Paramitas, the Gathering of Many Rivers

Chapter Thirteen

Rebazar Tarzs, Torchbearer of the Light and Sound

~❤~

How do you keep love in your heart when there is nothing but darkness around you? By blessing all that you encounter in your day, no matter what it is, bless it and watch the road disappear under your flying feet. This is how the Wise Ones completed their long and winding journeys -- by seeing nothing but the face of love in all that they encountered.

~❤~

The meaning of my name

Master Rebazar Tarzs:

"Rebazar" means "mountain man of strength, endurance and solitude", "Tarzs" means "of the high mountains". As such, I have lived my life in the remote altitudes of the Himalayas, where the searing drops from the mountain precipices have been my neighbors these past five hundred years. I was led to study with the great Milarepa during an out-of-body experience when he approached me and asked if I wanted to be his student. He was with another ancient sage, Methusula, who wanted me to learn the secret art of universal consciousness - to carry the conscience of the universe. He had chosen me as a candidate to bear the Torch of the Light and Sound because of my Inner strength and capacity for endurance.

The Torchbearer of the Light and Sound

I am The Torchbearer of the Light and Sound because that was the role I was best suited for in the grand scheme of universal plans. I am the one who holds the Rod of Power when there is no one assigned to the role of the Living Sehaji Master. Someone must "hold up" the conscience and life of the universe - similar to Atlas holding the world on his back. It is a role of ultimate endurance and dedication to the Living Flow of God's Power in the Lower Worlds before the First Grand Division. The Rod or Torch of the Light and Sound must always be held by a Living Master assigned by Sugmad, or complete darkness will descend upon the physical planes and all progress will come to a grinding halt as souls are put into a state of suspended animation. The Lower Worlds will go to sleep when there is no guiding light and God force to hold them up and give them life. And so the role of Torchbearer of the Light and Sound of God is one of tremendous responsibility and it has required that I stay within a material body as it is meant for a Living Master. This is the reason I have maintained a physical vehicle within the world of mankind for all these centuries.

Studying on the road to Mastership with Milarepa

Since a large part of my mission was to be the Torchbearer of the Light and Sound, I had to understand how the universe is kept in balance; and so we had many lessons and tours at Agam Des to study the secrets of keeping the universal wheels in motion and heading in the right direction in alignment with Sugmad's Divine Plan. I was taught to understand how past, present and future events could be manipulated and reconfigured to stay on the right path so that nothing would fall outside of the vision of the Sugmad for this grand experiment of Spirit. I have enjoyed overseeing the multi-faceted realities of the various planes of existence and their inhabitants. Their futures and karmic destinies were laid out before me like road maps and I could see the myriad possible outcomes of all the different directions and choices taken therein. It is a monumentally thrilling experience to be a Master of the Universe, but also a gravely responsible one. You cannot turn your back or close even one eye for one instant lest you miss a sidetrack that could start the dominos falling. And so I am always on "watch duty" and there is no changing of the guard for the One who holds the Torch of God.

The progression of the Light and Sound since Master Peddar Zaskq

The Light and Sound in the Lower Worlds moves forward and then backward, and then jumps forward again, going further than before so that there is always progress to be made. When Paul Twitchell started his mystery school, he was riding the forward movement of the Light and Sound - he had caught it at its crest like the height of an ocean wave before it crashes into the sea to take on new components and energy to form into an even higher wave. The higher the wave, the more it will dive and then gather forces to rise even higher when the cycle is over. This has been the pattern of the Light and Sound in the physical world. It had reached a median crest in the former path during the 1980's when there was a transfer of leadership; then it crested to a peak until the late 1990's when it began to dive again. Now it has experienced a resurgence of gathering forces with the leadership of Dan Rin and will reach another peak in 2010. Remember that each time the Light and Sound reaches a peak, it is higher than the one before and will continue that way until all souls are riding the highest crests back to the Sea of Love and Mercy. With each peak in waves, more souls are gathered and ride them home. So, the evolvement of the Light and Sound has increased in capacity to gather souls and impart wisdom and love to the Lower Worlds. It has peaked and crashed, but continues to gather more momentum with each dive and reaches ever higher into the God worlds with greater and greater power to bring this universe to its divine conclusion and ultimate destiny.

Physical body immortalization and food

I was assisted by the Master, Fubbi Quantz, who has taught many apprentices on the road to Mastership about the way of the God Eaters. I drink only purified water from the highest mountain springs and enjoy the occasional fruit or vegetable, plus flax seed bread or a cereal mush made with cornmeal, bran, oats, or rye; and also fermented libation. Eating is no longer a necessity for me, but my body "remembers" the act and process of taking in solid food and there is an emotional and societal enjoyment attached to it. Eating food is similar to the sexual drive in man; both can be controlled and maintained through the kundalini energy running through the spine. Man can live without bread and without sex as long as the "hunger" is satisfied through the proper use of the God force. This is an acquired art and demands great self-discipline and sacrifice, but the reward of the increase of divine love, drive, purpose and BLISS far outweighs any sense of "loss" the individual may feel. I hope this response has been helpful.

Passing the torch of Lightbearer

It is simply time to "pass the torch"; much like the Olympic runners who go the distance and expend their energy until a new entity with fresh forces can take over to insure that the torch stays lit and held high for all to see and gather strength from the sight. I have been running this race for a long, long time and the higher worlds beckon with greater responsibilities and joyous adventure. I have reached the finish line, so to speak, and am hanging up my "track shoes."

The Sugmad (God) has been in the process of creating new worlds and planets as yet uncharted and unheard of in the Lower Worlds; they require settlement and leadership. I will be one of the Founding Masters to these New Frontiers that will bring in a new race of beings and will be the birthplace for many souls yet to be given the divine spark of life from the Creator. This will keep me busy for many eons to come.

Mentoring today's God seekers

I prefer to work one-on-one with God seekers in the dream state in one of the classrooms in a Temple of Golden Wisdom such as those in Ekere Tere, Askleposis, and other places of learning in the God Worlds. Often, a God seeker makes an appointment with me while traveling in their soul body; this is done by calling my name from the Third Eye while in contemplation and I speak with the higher aspect of the individual. An appointment is made to meet with me in one of the Temples to address life and spiritual issues or to learn a specific spiritual skill or discipline. I used to conduct interplanetary seminars with a large audience from all over the cosmos, but now I prefer to work with souls on an individual basis. I enjoy the personal contact with them and am working especially closely with those souls who are slated for roles of spiritual leadership and those approaching Mastership status.

God seekers with disabilities

It is a life choice to take on a body with physical disabilities and illness; that is the first thing I discuss in counseling those who suffer with pain and disease. They have chosen this way of alleviating the "disease" of their karmic burden and debt to this world. It is a spiritual path in itself to bear illness, just as it is a path to care for the sick and dying, or to teach, heal, uplift and entertain others through writing, talks, books and movies. Those who choose the path of learning through illness become our most compassionate saints and martyrs. Christ Jesus had suffered great physical distress in past lives before taking on the role of a world savior. Mother Theresa was able to heal the open physical and spiritual wounds of the sick and dying souls in Calcutta because of her own experience with severe illness in the life previous to that of her role as comforter, healer, and saint. I always counsel those who come to me with illness to look upon it as the blessing of the angels to one who will overcome pain and suffering and become a source of great light, comfort and compassion to those who seek God's infinite Love and Mercy.

Our planet's environmental and spiritual balance

I have watched the deterioration of the ozone layer which is one of my greatest concerns. This is more than a protective shield from harmful ultra-violet sun rays; it literally shields the Earth from hostile alien vibrations sent out from invisible aircraft that are meant to invade the delicate infrastructure of the Earth's harmonic resonance.

In other words, this energetic invasion is meant to destroy what keeps the Earth alive as a planet and as a spiritual entity. I am currently working with the Green and Brown Robes to align the cosmic forces that work in harmony with nature and the elements to fortify the ozone layer and also form a magnetic shield around the Earth that will absorb hostile vibrations and render them harmless before ever reaching the planet itself. There is a new movement going on in your world called "Going Green" and this is part of my work with the Green and Brown Robed Orders. It is my desire to call attention to the need to go back to what is natural and healthy for this planet. Working to heal Earth from an organic level will also stimulate the spiritual balance of its inhabitants. While man is in a human body, there is no separation between organic and spiritual health and so this is my main focus of concern at this time to restore balance between them.

My mentoring of Master Peddar Zaskq

I taught him to master the art of time travel because I wanted him to accompany me as we visited various Masters during their lifetimes on Earth. I did not want him to channel the information as much as I wanted him to witness their lives first-hand like a journalist or reporter. He needed to be where the action was taking place and absorb the knowledge as it was given at the time. All that I taught him was taught to me by the Ancients; my method of learning from them was to time travel -- into the past and future -- and sit with them in person. I took on a physical body to walk with them during their incarnations on Earth and other planets and solar systems. This, to me, is the best way of learning and absorbing knowledge --

hands-on and in person with the Teachers. Once he mastered time travel, I taught Peddar Zaskq how to shift his consciousness into alignment with any source of wisdom he wished to absorb from any place or time in history. He had only to ask the question or call forth a person or historical event and the knowledge they contained would be transmitted to his conscious awareness and understanding. This is called one of Ten Powers of Soul which is elaborated in his book, "Letters to Gail III." This is how I taught him and this is why he was often accused of "plagiarism" when the truth of the matter is that he simply absorbed information as it was taking place or making history. I wanted to speed up the process and distribution of his teachings on Earth and this is how he was able to produce such a massive body of work in so short a time.

The high road to God

As you see the road to God-Realization stretched long and desolate before you, do not look from start to finish, and do not even look one step ahead, but watch your feet that move effortlessly by your love for Sugmad (God) and all that is within Its Mercy. It is your love for God that will move you forward and nothing else. There is no goal greater than that, to love and understand God. How do you keep love in your heart when there is nothing but darkness around you? By blessing all that you encounter in your day, no matter what it is, bless it and watch the road disappear under your flying feet. This is how the Wise Ones completed their long and winding journeys -- by seeing nothing but the face of love in all that they encountered. They did not look at the tiger's fangs but saw the grace of its movements and the beauty of its fighting spirit. They blessed its ability to tear them apart and honored the divine source of the power behind it. In this act of love, all tigers of the world bowed before them and let them pass unharmed. You can walk through the valley of darkness and wild beasts and see only the flicker of moonlight bouncing off a leaf. Keep your eyes on that spot of light; acknowledge only love and all dark and savage things will retreat from your path.

Herein follows a contemplative exercise to journey with Rebazar to his abode in the Himalayas for conversation and enlightenment:

1. Imagine yourself in sturdy hiking clothes and standing at the feet of the Himalayan mountains high in Tibet.

2. A guide approaches you with a llama in tow; climb aboard the llama and allow the guide to gently lead you on the path up the mountainside. It is a sunny and warm day and the sky is a deep, azure blue.

3. Breathe in the clean air and enjoy the feeling of going higher up the mountain of your consciousness. Presently, you can see the round dome of a white hut at the top of the trail and as you get closer, you can see me standing outside waving to you. I appear many ways to many people and so it is up to you how you wish to see me. Perhaps, in my traditional maroon robe and sandals with black hair and beard, it does not matter; what matters is the love you will see shining in my face.

4. When you have my image clearly before you, say this mantra and the whole picture will become animated

and "alive" - like a tapestry you can step into: **"RE-BA-ZAR-ALLA-TE."**

5. The rest of the contemplation is up to you; perhaps we are inside the hut having tea and conversation. Or perhaps I take your hand and we fly over the mountains to the God Worlds to visit a Temple of Wisdom. Or any number of scenarios that may be impressed upon you based on your needs and desires at the time. I am open to anything you need for your spiritual growth. Or simply say, **"Rebazar, take my hand and lead me where I most need to be at this time and tell me what I most need to know."**

Many blessings to the faithful, who seek the truth of God.

~ Epilogue ~

I found throughout the course of *Paramitas, the Gathering of Many Rivers*, countless areas of dialogue that could have expanded into what would represent itself as another book. It was a great privilege to speak with the various masters of different pathways of life. The diversity of reality and beliefs of this world is a direct reflection of God's Love for all life and Its acknowledgement that each culture has a set of unique needs and requirements of life-survival. Some of the subjects will be revisited in future literature for further elaboration and discussion. We exist within the fabric of infinity and one book will not capture the essence of some grey areas never discussed in other literature of The Light and Sound.

Paramitas, the Gathering of Many Rivers shows the convergence of how many walks of life move in parallel and converge as ONE. For there is only ONE GOD, ONE ULTIMATE REALITY and One TRUE GOAL for SOUL. Love God unconditionally and render the same freedom to your brothers and sisters of this Earth, and you will sail upon the Grace of Its love into the Sea of Love and Mercy.

I see this work as a doorway to other realms of understanding and a cornerstone of virgin territory waiting for spiritual conversation among God seekers of similar philosophy and bent. I deeply appreciate Rebazar Tarzs' coming forth to share with us his life-ideas and his spiritual mission as the Torchbearer of The Light and Sound of God. He has been an inspiration to me and others throughout the entirety of my life. In drawing closure to the vibration of this book, I bid you my unyielding love, commitment and support on this spiritual road to Self-Realization and God-Realization. Blessed Be.

~ *Sri Michael Owens*

For more information,
you are invited to visit:
www.thewayoftruth.org

Paramitas, the Gathering of Many Rivers

~ Glossary ~

A

Akashic record. Records of significant events in each soul's earthly life, maintained as files in the Hall of Records in the Causal Plane.

B

Best-Laid-Plans Sugmad's dream for its creation of the universe and all life forms; a dream in which sleeping souls tested, tried and proven through the fires of purification, eventually awaken. Once fully awake, Sugmad's children see each other as brother and sister, person to person, nation to nation. Love, peace, harmony and Sugmad's abundance reign.

C

Contemplation This is an active form of engaging the mind in activity aligned with soul, and in this way, differs from prayer and meditation.

D (none)

E

Emotional body The sheath relegated to the Astral Plane which holds our emotions.

Ego A part of the mind, ego's purpose is survival. Too often seduced by power, in actuality, the ego is like a ping-pong ball when compared to the sun.

Ekere Tere The spiritual city newly created to cleanse Africa from the black magic that has plagued it for centuries. Africa is the heart of the Earth; when Africa heals, Mother Earth can heal too.

F

Faith Is the inner, indomitable knowing that Sugmad's will is supreme, always harmonious, and filled with love; and that the universe belongs to and is itself an aspect of Sugmad's love.

G

Grand Council Headed by the ancient Sage, Milarepa, the Grand Council is comprised of Olden Ones of a Holy Order that precedes the dream of Sugmad. They originate from the Nameless One, the Most High, and oversee the outworking of Best Laid Plans.

God-Absorption Involves seeing, knowing and being a son or daughter of Sugmad. It is the ultimate reunification with Sugmad such that when you move, Sugmad moves.

God-Realization The cellular recognition, ignited from within, that you are a part of God.

H

Honor Includes the qualities of trustworthiness, loyalty, and devotion.

"Hauntings" These are often the phantoms of lingering thoughts created by the former inhabitants of the environments.

I

Initiations Each Initiation represents a milestone in the soul's life and indicates how far she or he has come and how far she or he has to go to reach the shores of the sea of Love and Mercy. Initiations sever the bonds that hold participants tied to the Lower Worlds so they can progress in unfoldment and enter the true Worlds of God.

J (none)

K

Karma Also known as the Law of Cause and effect, karma is the law by which soul reaps the rewards or experiences the consequences of prior actions, even from past lives, whether soul remembers them or not.

L

Lavender Robe This is a specially created energetic path in which a highly Secret Order operates at the discretion of the Most High.

Life Contract The agreement a soul makes before incarnating which is negotiated with the Lords of Karma for the soul to engage in life experiences necessary for its unfoldment.

Light and Sound These are the primary emanations from Sugmad that constitute the Life Force, source of all life and All That Is.

Love Is the indefinable yet intrinsic essence of what Sugmad is. Love is also wisdom, as wisdom is love. Love is the foundation of all life; without it, there would be nothing but darkness.

Lower Worlds These are the worlds below the Soul Plane which are: the Etheric, Mental, Causal, Astral, and Physical.

M

The Master Language This is the intuitive communication link between the heart charkas of every being in existence. Here is where the thoughts of the teacher go directly into the heart of the student, bypassing ego and mind.

Mental Plane The mental realm or mind without physical brain stuff, was made to take the intuitive impulses and step them down a few notches more. The Mental Plane includes the Etheric, however the Etheric is of a higher vibratory quality and sits directly below the Soul Plane.

N

Nampak This is a spiritual or angelic way station for those who have crossed over under traumatic conditions.

Non-power The non-power is the receiver, the receptacle of Sugmad's Power. To experience the non-power, one must achieve true detachment with full loving awareness.

O (none)

P

Physical Plane The Physical Plane was created for souls to experience gross and corporeal beauty and pain from its sensory apparatus. As the lowest Plane, it completes Sugmad's playground and grand experiment for the education and evolution of souls, sparks of Sugmad's own Self, units of Sugmad's awareness.

Prophesy Prophesy reaches into the innermost truth behind all things and is the hidden Eye of God that can only be revealed by a master of the Ninth Circle or above.

Q *(none)*

R

Red Dragon Order The Red Dragon Order consists of those great souls committed to their mission of protecting the Light and Sound. They guard vortices and otherwise defend and protect actors and actions harmonious with Sugmad's Best laid Plans.

S

Sanskaras These are magnetic energy wrappings coiling around the body that identify each soul as having a unique magnetic resonance.

Sat Nam He is the God of the Fifth Plane who is the first true manifestation of the Supreme God of the universe.

Self-Realization This is the first stage of soul's entrance into the heavenly worlds as it journeys into these worlds on beingness and pure love. Here the aspirant recognizes her or himself as Soul, not as the lower bodies soul uses to gain experiences in the Lower Worlds.

Service Means taking action motivated by love and goodwill, according to the prompting of one's own heart. True service the giving of loving actions with no expectation of receiving in return.

Shamballa The City of Peace and Harmony, it is the place where the Great White Brotherhood has its meeting ground and is the foundation for the propagation of peace to unify all parts of the world.

Soul Soul is a singular unit of awareness from the living breath of Sugmad..

Sugmad This constitutes a pure name for God, the Creator of this universe and all life forms.

Surrender Is the act of letting go of all attachments and the grip of ego. This creates an opening for the Most High to enter in and guide your life.

T

Temples of Wisdom These are Inner Temples where spiritual training, purification and the imparting of secrets occur. These spiritual temples are contained within vortices of varying degrees that transmit frequencies coming from the highest realms.

Third Eye A spot located about half an inch above and between the eyebrows that corresponds to the location of the pineal gland. Spiritual movies or visions can be seen when one's eyes are closed and attention is gently placed there.

The Power of Theta Similar to sound therapy, the Theta Power channels the Sound Current and can completely restructure the electrical makeup of the human body and heal it.

The Torchbearer of the Light and Sound The Torchbearer is Rebazar Tarzs, he is the one who holds the Rod of Power when there is no one assigned to the role of the Living Sehaji Master.

$\mathcal{U}$

Universal Soul Movement This is a profound yet simple movement of consciousness from the realm of the ordinary physical reality to the higher and finer aspects of divine consciousness.

Uncharted lands The Uncharted lands are the inner landscapes of spiritual consciousness. These may be assessed only through a master of very high merit to guide you.

$\mathcal{V}$

Vanity Vanity is the aspect of ego that represents the lost soul who wanders aimlessly looking for itself in superficial gratification of the senses.

$\mathcal{W}$

The White Brotherhood Known as the Great White Brotherhood, its members are the Keepers of the Flame of Peace among men and women on Earth. Working with the Angelic Hierarchies, the White Brotherhood can move the tides of whole nations toward finding peaceful resolutions to their stormy seas of warfare and strife.

$\mathcal{X}$ *(none)*

$\mathcal{Y}$ *(none)*

$\mathcal{Z}.$ *(none)*

~ ♥ ~

Paramitas, the Gathering of Many Rivers

Index

A

V

W

~ ♥ ~

Paramitas, the Gathering of Many Rivers

Other Books
by
Michael Edward Owens

(Sri Michael Owens)

The Way of Truth Eternal ~ Book I

The ancient words of truth are written in the sacred pages of the Holy Books of the Light and Sound. These sacred writings are contained and housed and held and protected in sacred temples of light where they are guarded by the members of the Sehaji Hierarchies. As the universe unfolds and progresses, these works are given and revealed in physical form below to create a grounding point for the vortex of their energy and power so that it might be found and felt and experienced within the realms where it is needed.

And so, this is the first of these luminous works given to man by the hand of the Sehaji, Dan Rin, the current Living Sehaji Master, and its words and truth are vital because they do address of critical points of confluence, which previously had been blocked and obstructed and had prevented the clear flows of energy that are necessary and required by those groups of Souls currently incarnated on Earth and within the other realms and seeking in their progression to move together onward on the path.

Paramitas, the Gathering of Many Rivers

And so, *The Way of Truth Eternal, Book I* has been sent and given to all Souls to open up their hearts and to aid their understanding and their movement on the path and return to higher realms above.

Sri Michael Owens

Babaji, the Beginning Has No End

It is my privilege and pleasure to write this introduction on the dialogues of Babaji. I have admired this great avatar throughout my many lifetimes. He has been a dear friend and mentor whose help has been invaluable in my leadership of the path of Light and Sound, The Way of Truth. Babaji taught me how to examine and use the chakras in the movement of consciousness outside the body called, "Universal Soul Movement."

Babaji also initiated the awakening of my spiritual training in the physical realms. It was this great avatar that introduced me to my later mentors and teachers of old: Kadmon, Agnotti, and Milati. These spiritual masters have been my advisors since the beginning of my spiritual journey.

It was Babaji's intention to give those who know and love him a book that provides creative responses to the issues of love, family, work and daily life. Consequently, this book discusses spirituality in a way unique to other books on Babaji. What I found extremely effective for daily living were the contemplative exercises he offers in this book to expand the God seeker's sphere of love and knowledge. The words used as mantras (words of prayer) are phonetically charged with love and Light and Sound. The meaning of certain phraseology in the contemplative exercises is written to transcend the intervention of the mind. I have used terminology entrenched in the olden ways of the spiritual, like Sugmad, also known as God. This term was used due to its structural integrity, and it has never been profaned in human language and verbal communication. Thus, the vibration to the word "Sugmad" has never been depleted or violated.

As the Living Teacher of The Way of Truth, I am called a Sehaji Master. The term "Sehaji" means, "Master of the Celestial Seas," alluding to the Great Sea of Love and Mercy, the home of God's consciousness. This book was not intended to recruit or to propagandize the teachings of The Way of Truth, but there are references made to it throughout this book. Babaji's spiritual teachings and those of The Way of Truth were inevitable to intersect with one another. In essence, the foundations of both ways of life are integrally related to the beauty of God's love for all life and the freedom of Soul.

I believe you will find this book spiritually uplifting and of practical use in matters of spiritual inquiry. Many doors of perception and adventure await the God seeker who reads this book, uses the contemplative exercises, and follows the path inside this book. The truth unveiled in this book is like the light shining brightly at the end of the tunnel.

Sri Michael Owens

Ekere Tere, City of Light

This book is a compilation of my spiritual studies with various teachers who are now teaching at Ekere Tere, the City of Light. This city was constructed in the High Astral Plane above the capital city of Abuja, Nigeria. Ekere Tere is a place of learning, specifically designed to forefront the newly calibrated teachings of The Way of Truth, to eradicate the imbalanced presence of black magic in the world and to open the spiritual doors of Africa's Renaissance.

The Way of Truth, the new path of the Light and Sound, stands as the spiritual guardian of all ways of life through the higher learning of Ekere Tere, the City of Light. The Way of Truth affirms the vibratory essence of the Light and Sound in every theology and life-path that holds unconditional love and non-judgment as its foundation. The unitary consciousness of all life is cohesively welded together by Sugmad's love and it is this love which is serving all life as the driving force of existence. It is our heart and its ability to connect with the eternal fabric of Sugmad's plan that opens our Universal Soul Movement to the inexplicable bliss beyond the ken of human eyes. Our heart is the key.

Paramitas, the Gathering of Many Rivers

There are many paths to God and each soul must choose the course of their own spiritual unfoldment. This is Soul's eternal right. Soul was placed in a physical shell to understand its immortal gift of existence and to learn in a human laboratory of communication and cooperation, and ultimately to expand its consciousness of love and begin its Universal Soul Movement home.

Within the contents of this book, there is spoken dialogue which presents limitless knowledge to the seekers who want God-Realization in this lifetime. The spoken word of these Masters gives the reader a great opportunity to partake of the love I felt throughout the years of my spiritual training. It is my hope you will try the spiritual exercises to see if they fulfill your spiritual needs. To those seeking to see and visit Ekere Tere, you have my love and Darshan. A great adventure awaits each of you.

Many Blessings,
Sri Michael Owens

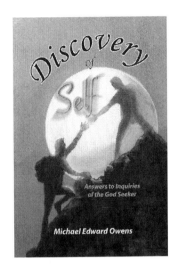

Discovery of Self

Upon careful reflection and examination of my life, I found myself looking at life with utmost indebtedness to many Spiritual Masters, whose help and guidance have been simply invaluable. To look at my accomplishments is to give credit to those who have spent endless hours teaching me the basics of human survival and spiritual knowledge. I cannot tell you of the loving patience rendered to me through my years of learning and contemplation on the higher aspects of the spiritual life. I found that each of us has a childlike seeker festering inside of us who is yearning for spiritual growth. I was a stubborn student, often having to learn the issues of life the hard way, and in many instances a helping hand was there to pick me up off the ground. I remember the first time I sat with a spiritual master of high note in his mud hut sipping a rather unusual tasting tea as he expressed his views of life, existence and the beautiful journey awaiting each Soul as they progressed toward the pure spiritual worlds of God. This experience was the first of many Universal Soul Movement adventures I had "outside the physical body." I still cannot believe how my journey into the true spiritual life began with a book I read in 1975, *In My Soul, I am Free*, by Brad Steiger.

A qualitative change in life can come from the simplest of elements. I have found in my brief span of living in this life that each person is a unit of God's awareness and is seeking to express this to other human beings. It is the nature of human beings to inquire, question, and pursue answers to longstanding situations and emotional crises. What we gather from this world and how we apply it to our quality of living is the standard by which we weigh the merits of the spiritual life. To truly live and endure with dignity is to acknowledge the beauty of all creation as a unified whole. This book has been written with the confirmed reality that each person is searching for new ways to improve his or her life, and is seeking new ways to express their love to others in their personal and impersonal environments. As long as we live, we are tied to a never-ending connection of decisions to be made. It is important to know if our answers fill the empty cup of our inquiries and demands placed upon our plate. *Each question embodies its own answer; after all, this universe is a unity of contradicting forces-in-action.* The purpose of this book is to give the seeker of truth spiritual methods to build individual life strategies for survival in this constantly changing world. As individuals, we must have direction in defining and prioritizing our sacred values and beliefs. Each individual has their own reality and their own way of relating this internal process to others. To test the mettle of what I have mentioned, ask yourself what are the principles and values you believe in, and are you living by those standards? Whatever you know and believe those elements to be, they are not written in stone. This world is in constant flux, and we must move with it to make sense of the world we live in. Our awareness of what we know changes and thus our beliefs and morals change. Beyond the pendulum of negative and positive polarities of existence lies the Pure God Worlds of Beingness that can be individually experienced by the seeker within each of us. Critical views on the entirety of living will change if you, as the seeker, build from your inner sanctum first and your outer world secondly. No one sees the inside of you but yourself, so make the decision to build what you want from this reference point. The outer world is a reflection of the architectural design beginning from this Inner Development. My book offers different rock and mortar to build thy house.

Each of us is born into this life like a child left in a learning laboratory. We must concern ourselves with what materials we feed our minds and souls. Consequently, the teachers we choose to embellish our lives with represent an important as well as critical step in our unfoldment. A mentor of high merit once said to me that good teachers understand they can only help their students to remember what they already know. Thus, the teacher points the way for the true seeker to determine his or her own individual path. This is the process of true spiritual instruction.

Sri Michael Owens

Notes

~ ♥ ~

Paramitas, the Gathering of Many Rivers

Notes

~ ♥ ~

Notes

~ ♥ ~

Paramitas, the Gathering of Many Rivers

Notes

~ ♥ ~

Notes

~ ♥ ~

Notes

~ ♥ ~

Notes

~ ♥ ~

Notes

~ ♥ ~

5941559R0

Made in the USA
Charleston, SC
24 August 2010